A MAN FORBID

A reading of
Shakespeare's *Macbeth*

Matt Simpson

GREENWICH EXCHANGE
LONDON

Greenwich Exchange, London

First published in Great Britain in 2003
All rights reserved

A Man Forbid – a reading of Shakespeare's *Macbeth*
© Matt Simpson 2003

Printed and bound by Q3 Digital/Litho, Loughborough
Tel: 01509 213456
Typesetting and layout by Albion Associates, London
Tel: 020 8852 4646
Cover design by December Publications, Belfast
Tel: 028 90352059

Cover photograph © John Timbers / Arena PAL

Greenwich Exchange Website: www.greenex.co.uk

ISBN 1-871551-69-2

for Gael

I would like to express my thanks to Angela Topping and John Farrell with whom I discussed some of the points raised in this book, to Dorothy O'Hanlon and Norman Payne for providing useful information, but above all to Professor John Lucas who kindly read the first draft and helped me sharpen up some of my observations.

Between the acting of a dreadful thing
And the first motion, all the interim is
Like a phantasma or a hideous dream,
The genius, and all the mortal instruments
Are then in council; and the state of man,
Like to a little kingdom, suffers then
The nature of an insurrection.

Julius Caesar

A peace above all earthly dignities,
A still and quiet conscience.

King Henry the Eighth

Thus conscience doth make cowards of us all,
And thus the native hue of resolution
Is sicklied o'er with the pale cast of thought.

Hamlet

My conscience hath a thousand several tongues,
And every tongue brings in a several tale,
And every tale condemns me for a villain.

Richard III

There is a middle road between understanding nothing
and understanding too much, a juste milieu *which poets*
instinctively respect more than critics.

Montale

Contents

Expense Of Time – By Way Of A Preface

There is an obvious difference between audience involvement in the dynamics of performance and the experience afforded by reading. In performance we take part in a communal activity, shared between actors and audience – in other words, in a largely uninterrupted process. In reading we can do what we like, pause when we like, determine for ourselves the pace of what is normally a solitary activity; we can consider 'meanings', become aware of structure, repetitions – words, phrases, images, motifs – all of which is interesting, of course, but important only if the activity enhances, deepens our experience of performance, of what the play was written to do.

Nothing, however, is definitive: there is no set of answers that will 'explain' the play; and each performance is an interpretation, a 'view'. But that doesn't mean that we shouldn't try hard to understand what the language is doing, what sets of assumptions – sometimes missing to us – with which the play may seem to be working. We need to exercise our historical imaginations. For example, it is necessary to see the events enacted in a Shakespeare play as *sub specie aeternitas* or, as I put it later, to judge what is happening in the context of eternity.

Macbeth is a play obsessively concerned, as I hope to show, with time. It requires us to try to see human beings as, in the words of John Donne, "a little world made cunningly of Elements and an Angelic sprite" – in other words, paradoxical beings who share qualities with the animals (lower or bestial parts) and with the angels (higher self or soul). Life is a struggle between these two – our good angels and our bad. There is both this world and the world of Grace.

Macbeth is 'about' (in the words of Sonnet 129) the "expense of spirit in a waste of shame". It is 'about' what Macbeth does with time and what times does with him. The world he inhabits is subject to change, growth, decay, which can only occur in the dimension of time. On the evidence of Elizabethan literature generally, mutability was for writers of the time a central theme. Human beings were thrust into the world of time and death by Adam's Original Sin. In his poem *Nosce Teipsum* of 1599 Sir John Davies writes:

> God first made angels bodiless, pure minds,
>   Then other things, which mindless bodies be:
> Last he made man, th'horizon 'twixt both kinds
>   In whom we do the world's abridgement see.

The world of Grace was not subject to change and death: it was a world of harmony and everlastingness; it was the hoped-for destination of the virtuous. This is therefore, so to speak, a form of the future outside time: *sub specie aeternitas*. And we must not, of course, forget its counterpart, the destination of unredeemed sinners.

The way we perceive time is a necessary part of our consideration of the play. Our modern perceptions are usefully summed up in the following extract from *The Emperor's Mind* by Roger Penrose:

> Central to our feelings of awareness is the sensation of the progression of time. We *seem* to be moving ever forward, from a definite past into an uncertain future. The past is over, we feel, and there is nothing to be done with it. It is unchangeable, and in a certain sense, it is 'out there' still. Our present knowledge of it may come from our records, our memory traces, and our deductions from them, but we do not tend to doubt the *actuality* of the past. The past was one thing and can (now) *be* only one thing. What has happened has happened, and there is now nothing whatever that we, nor anyone else can do about it! The future, on the other hand, seems yet undetermined. It could turn out to be one thing or it could turn out to be another. Perhaps this 'choice' is fixed completely by physical laws, or perhaps partly by our own decisions (or by God); but this 'choice' seems still there to be made. There appear to be merely *potentialities* for whatever the 'reality' of the future may actually resolve itself to be. As we consciously perceive time to pass, the most immediate part of that vast and

seemingly undetermined future becomes realized as actuality, and thus makes its entry into a fixed past. Sometimes we have the feeling that *we* even have been personally 'responsible' for somewhat influencing that choice of particular potential future which in fact becomes realized, and made permanent in the actuality of the past. More often, we feel ourselves to be helpless spectators – perhaps thankfully relieved of responsibility – as, inexorably, the scope of the determined past edges its way into an uncertain future.

Our conception of time is as something fluid and therefore problematic, but many of the considerations in the above extract can be used to cast light upon what happens in *Macbeth* along with our understanding of how Shakespeare's audience saw things.

Our modern view of Nature, too, needs adjustment if we are to understand the play. Our attitude has been conditioned by the Romantics, resulting in the popular view that it is something external – trees, fields, waterfalls, flowers – something set in opposition to man-made things, in particular cities and urban living. In Shakespeare's time it invariably meant the whole of God's hierarchically arranged creation.

It is the work of the Devil to undermine this order. In the early play, *Gorboduc*, first acted in 1561, we have the lines:

> ... Nature hath her order and her course,
> Which being broken doth corrupt the state
> Of minds and things, even in the best of all.
> (Act I, scene 2, 220-2)

This is exactly what happens in *Macbeth*. The Elizabethan theologian, Richard Hooker, (whom I quote at greater length later) wrote "Obedience of creatures unto the Law of Nature is the stay of the whole world".

A further point to do with time: *Macbeth* is set in the ancient past. The historical Macbeth died in 1057. Shakespeare's audience had a different attitude to history from our own more scientifically-aided constructions. For them History was largely a pageant of exempla, a narrative of good and bad lives, from which lessons could be drawn. In *Macbeth* they witnessed, as I suggested earlier, "the expense of spirit in a waste of shame".

And to complicate perception of time further: they were witnessing a version of events purporting to have happened half-a-millennium earlier which had connections with their own present and future through their newly-anointed monarch. And they were doing so in what I later call 'theatre-time': history compressed into a two-hour-long play (often played without an interval, thus accentuating the sense of its inexorability) – in the afternoon – in an open-air theatre – watching terrifying things happening on stage – at night.

I have used the expression 'historical imagination'. This does not imply an attempt to arrive at a reductive 'explanation' of the play's concerns. I believe it is important to try and learn what we can about Shakespeare's language and imagine a general context for it. I am not claiming that contextualising in this way is the answer to our understanding, simply (as far as we can be certain) an enabling element in it: I am fully aware that Shakespeare's plays take on different 'meanings' at different times. It is a truism for instance that every generation has its 'Hamlet'; it is true that we talk of Geilgud's or Olivier's or Branagh's 'Hamlet' etc., in the same way as we talk of Klemperer's or Harnoncourt's or Rattle's Beethoven. In other words Shakespeare and Beethoven are not fixed entities. I have no wish to turn them into museum pieces. Quite the contrary. The process of reading and re-reading is always one of discovery, of venturing into regions where it helps to have made some effort to learn a little of the language.

1

Firstlings

In Robert Nye's hilarious, Rabelaisian novel *The Late Mr Shakespeare*, we are presented with a wonderfully outrageous, highly fictionalised (what else, since we know so little about him?) account of Shakespeare's life as seen through the eyes of one Robert Reynolds alias the aged and garrulous Pickleherring, former comic actor, writing his story in a room above a London brothel some time after the Restoration of 1660. We have to wait till chapter 87 to learn about the writing of *Macbeth*. There Pickleherring identifies the witches as Agnes Thomson, Violet Leys and Janet Wishart as named in James I's *News from Scotland* and at whose trial in 1596 the king himself was in attendance.

Pickleherring goes on to tell us how Agnes Thomson and other witches went to sea in sieves, danced and sang, whilst the master of the coven, Giles Duncan, "played upon a Jew's trump" and how at the trial Agnes Thomson confessed that:

> 'she took a black toad and did hang the same up by the heels three days and gathered venom as it dropped and fell from it in an oyster shell'. She also took a cat and christened it which caused such a tempest that the vessel perished 'wherein was sundry jewels and rich gifts which should have been presented to the now Queen of Scotland'. The ship in which James sailed would have met the same fate if the King's 'faith had not prevailed above their intentions'. All this you can find for yourselves, good readers, in that silly *News from Scotland*.

He is in doubt that both this account and the King himself are 'silly', and after admitting he has no idea what Mr Shakespeare thought of the King, he however says: "I do know that he wrote *Macbeth* in part to please him".

1

He relates how Shakespeare's Company played in various places in Scotland, once before the King and once before the Queen. Shakespeare's sojourn in Scotland, he asserts, tells us to what extent "*Macbeth* is soaked in WS's experience" of the country:

> Banquo's first question 'How far is't called to Forres?' sounds rather more Scotch than English to my ear. QUELL for murder, SKIRR for search, LATCH instead of catch, GRUEL for broth, SLAB for sticky, CRIBBED for enclosed, all these are Northern words which Shakespeare uses only in *Macbeth.* The receptiveness of his ear was quite remarkable. I was in lodgings with him in Inverness, for example, and our hostess remarked approvingly of the porridge which she had boiled for us that it was *thick and slab* – the phrase went straight into the Scottish play, used of the contents of the witches' cauldron.

Here we are in what *The Hitch-Hiker's Guide to the Galaxy* calls Improbability Drive but I have started this way simply because the novel's amusing quirkiness and the compelling earthiness of Pickleherring's view can usefully be set against the off-putting image of Shakespeare inherited from 19th century bardolatry – that of the Immortal Genius, the superhuman Bard. Of course, there is very little likelihood Shakespeare ever visited Scotland and suffered a Mrs MacDiarmid's porridge (any more than he fought as a soldier in the Netherlands or went to sea with Francis Drake) but he did read Holinshed's *Chronicles* and he did base a play called *Macbeth* on what he found there. And it is true that, after a period of political and religious anxiety, England was relieved to have a new monarch – albeit one who came from a dubious Scotland and who had been on the throne for two years when the play was first staged at the Globe Theatre in 1606. King James was intelligent and literate and had indeed written books on witches – which Nye's Pickleherring, along with other contemporary documents, has obviously read. This is not to imply, of course, that Shakespeare himself had read them.

I doubt Shakespeare wrote the play *for* James I – even though the king was an enthusiast and a production was put on at Court in honour of the visit of the King of Denmark. Those who believe the play was written with the particular aim of flattering the King point to the fact that in the first year of his reign the new monarch privileged

Shakespeare's company (then the Lord Chamberlain's Men) by conferring on it the title of the King's Men. They point to the setting in Scotland, the incorporation of witchcraft, the references to the Gunpowder Plot, to Banquo's non-complicity in the murder of Duncan, and to the fact that in Act IV, scene 1 the vision of a line of kings extending from Banquo's son to a king with "two-fold balls and treble sceptres", symbolising the twice-crowned James. A.L. Rowse in his *Shakespeare the Elizabethan* tells us that there "had been an upsurge of popularity for the new royal house on their deliverance" (i.e. from the Gunpowder Plot) "which the dramatist was quick to take advantage of".

Be that as it may, I prefer to think of Shakespeare legitimately (i.e. not obsequiously) cashing in (he was, after all, earning his living attracting audiences) on topicality: the curiosity and anxieties (and the relief of knowing the problem of the succession had been solved) of Londoners about their new monarch and where he all-hailed from. I am inclined to the view expressed by Jonathan Bate in *The Genius of Shakespeare* that "Flattery of King James is marginal to the dramatic life of *Macbeth*": the play, he points out, is about Macbeth, not about Banquo, the king's ancestor – though Shakespeare thought it appropriate to make Banquo a somewhat more virtuous-seeming character than the one found in his immediate source. The incorporation of topical material does not of necessity presuppose that Shakespeare was flatteringly bolstering James' self-image or seeking favours.

It is a fact that the 17th century was nastily paranoid about witches and killed off thousands of men and women thought to have made alliances with the Devil. Shakespeare's bringing Scottish witches on to the stage was like Marlowe's, a decade earlier, terrifying audiences with Mephistopheles and Lucifer in *Doctor Faustus* and Machiavelli in *The Jew of Malta* with undeniably powerful dramatic impact: a glimpse of the forbidden, a vicarious encounter with agents of evil who "oftentimes, to win us to our harm,/ … tell us truths,/ Win us with honest trifles, to betray's/ In deepest consequence." The witches in *Macbeth* are associated with the appalling sin of regicide – which the ghost in *Hamlet* describes as "Murder most foul, as in the best it is". Ghosts, witches, fairies, devils were believed in as realities, not as poetic fancies.

3

It is also true, as Bate says, that *Macbeth* "is a Gunpowder play through and through". There are overt references to the attempt on 5th November 1605 to blow up (in the hope of unleashing a Catholic uprising) the Palace of Westminster with the King and Parliament present. The plot involved Midlands families which Shakespeare must have known: this idea excites those commentators who now think the poet a covert Catholic into imagining sympathies and anxieties at work in him whilst writing. (Anthony Holden suggests that the play's "obsessive theme of sleep or lack of it" may even be connected with Shakespeare's own sleeplessness knowing that papist families were being persecuted). On the other hand, it is, perhaps again, more a matter of topicality – allusion to what everyone in London was talking about at the time. One of the play's major motifs is that of equivocation – something explored more fully later. For the moment, let's deal with the play's most obviously direct references to the subject. In Act II, scene 2, the porter tells us that an equivocator is one "that could swear in both the scales against either scale, who committed treason/ enough for God's sake, yet could not equivocate to/ heaven". Another is in Act IV, scene 2, when Macduff's young son, asks his mother "What is a traitor?" and receives the reply "Why, one that swears and lies". The matter being referred to in both these passages is the Jesuit doctrine that allowed a prisoner to disguise the truth in order to escape incrimination: the doctrine of equivocation. The last conspirator to be tried for treason in this case was one Father Garnet who had written a treatise on the subject. It should be noted that the play is at pains to condemn equivocation and treats it from a strictly Protestant standpoint, which sees it as a submission to the forces of evil – something, of course, witches were said to do. In Act V, scene 5 Macbeth says in despair "I pull in resolution, and begin/ To doubt the equivocation of the fiend/ That lies like truth." The porter tells us that "much drink may be said to be an equivocator with lechery".

It is not necessarily wrong, however, to see the proper subject of the play as Scotland – a need to exorcise barbarity from its history through the promise of a line of kings running from Banquo to James. It is no accident that the play ends with Malcolm creating earls, "the first that ever Scotland/ In such an honour named" – a conferring of honours to which James was prone (and for which, in some quarters he was criticised) handed out especially to his Scottish followers once he had ascended the throne of England. It is also interesting to note that the "healing benediction" (the royal touch said to cure the 'Evil' or scrofula) which Malcolm reverently attributes to the English king, Edward the Confessor, in Act IV, scene 3, was something of which James was deeply sceptical, at first refusing to continue the ceremony and only reluctantly agreeing to do so with the persuasion that it was a custom maintained in France. Why would Shakespeare recommend to the king something for which he was known to have no appetite – unless of course he was reflecting public opinion and making a plea for its continuation?

It is worth remembering that James' father, Lord Darnley, had been murdered before he had reached the age of 21, and that his murder was associated with the use of gunpowder. James had become King of Scotland at the age of seven months and his first decade was, in the words of Alan Stewart in his biography, *The Cradle King*, "one of the most bitter and bloody periods in Scottish history". For a description of Darnley's death and of the execution of James' mother by Elizabeth I in the same year, a further account may be found in Antonia Fraser's *Mary Queen of Scots*. Concerning the execution of his mother, James wrote to Elizabeth admitting to her that "would God she might see the inward parts of my heart where she should see a great jewel of honesty towards her, locked up in a coffer of perplexity". Treason was part of James' family history and an awareness of these events would have been present in at least some of the play's original audience ... and it was for this audience, and not primarily James, Shakespeare was writing.

Popular imagination of the time tended to see Scotland as outside the civilised pale, a warrior culture of feuding clans – beautifully mirrored in the great Japanese director Kurosawa's filmed Samurai version of *Macbeth* entitled *The Throne of Blood* – a harsh mist-filled terrain of brooding superstition, caves harbouring wild men and witches. G.M. Trevelyan in *English Social History* says that for Chaucer Scotland was "an unknown, distant, barbarous land – much further off than France – 'far in the North, I cannot tellen where'". To John Fordun, in the same century, the men of the Highlands were "a savage and untamed people, rude and independent, given to rapine and ease-living".

The more sophisticated among Shakespeare's contemporaries would know that Scotland consisted of two areas: the Highlands where, as one observer (John Major in 1521) wrote, the Gaelic-speaking "Wild Scots" lived, "full of mutual dissensions, and war rather than peace"; then there were the more civilised Lowlands, where Major tells us the "householding Scots" lived. But complicating these was the Border Country where, according to Trevelyan, on "these roadless fells, society consisted of mounted clans of farmer-warriors, at feud among themselves and at war with the Scots". "This state of things," he says, "outlasted the Tudors. Only after the union of crowns on the head of James Stuart had made an end of Border war (1603) did peaceful manor houses begin to rise beside the castles and peel towers of the north ... The peculiar spirit of Scottish society ... was utterly unintelligible to the English mind until Sir Walter Scott's novels retrospectively afforded the key." Even in the 18th century the English attitude was that Scotland was virtually outside nature: in Trevelyan's words, a place where "primeval instincts and customs were still strong in the land of mountains and moors, and yet unconquered nature". Stewart writes of how the King's wish to unite England and Scotland was met by opposition from English MPs, whom he quotes as expressing astonishment "that any ear could be lent for joining a good and fertile country to one poor and a barren, and in a manner disgraced by nature; and for associating frank and honest men with such as were beggars, proud and generally traitors and rebels to their King".

It could be that Shakespeare was flattering James to the extent of bringing Scotland, as it were, on side – by slaying the Macbeth dragon ("this dead butcher, and his fiend-like Queen") and distorting history to honour James' ancestry and thus legitimise the Stuart dynasty (though when we come to look more closely at Banquo's character we may find this idea of a sanitised hero not quite so simple). The same may be said of the persecution and extirpation of village midwives and herbalists branded as witches – the deliberate eradication and exorcising of (to use Lady Macbeth's word) *ill-ness* – a word that powerfully fuses both moral (as in *ill*-natured) and medical meanings. In this regard, the play can be seen as an expression of hope – the accommodation by England of a Scottish heir to the throne.

Of course, much of this is speculative. As John Wain has written, topicality is "never more than one-seventh of the iceberg that shows above the surface". Shakespeare was more concerned with shaping events for optimal dramatic effect and we must keep reminding ourselves not to attribute to him thoughts and opinions his characters utter in contexts that are fictional, any more than we should accept Nye's Pickleherring's gossiping as literal truth.

2

The Seeds Of Time

In Shakespeare's principal source, Holinshed's *Chronicles*, King Duncan is in fact far from being the elderly sainted figure we find in the play; he is young and an inept ruler, murdered by Macbeth and Banquo as co-conspirators; Shakespeare makes use of quite a different murder for his story: that of King Duff by Donwald, persuaded to the deed by his wife; the sleepless nights of King Kenneth are perhaps also put to use. As for the Weird Sisters – what a transformation of Holinshed's "goddesses of destiny or else some nymphs or fairies endued with knowledge of prophecy by their necromantical science" Shakespeare made.

It is not without interest that Macbeth was – in so far as we can trust early Scottish accounts – a historical figure, who ruled his country successfully and not without respect for 17 years (Sigmund Freud thought that Shakespeare's ignoring of this – in John Wain's paraphrase – "does not allow time for him to become aware of the curse of sterility that has followed his wife's dreadful prayer, *unsex me here*"); and it is a historical fact that he was not Lady Macbeth's first husband (a point to be contemplated, not without a realisation of some obvious hazard, later). She married him in 1032. The historical Lady Macbeth's name was Gruoch and she had been previously married to the chieftain of Moray, whose name was Gillacogmain and, incidentally, in the complicated internecine way of clan feuding, had slain Findlaech, Macbeth's father, in 1020. This first marriage produced a son, Lulach (also killed by Malcolm). The Duncan of the play (there were several of that name) succeeded his grandfather in 1034. but, according to *Scotland from Earliest Times to 1603* by W. Croft Dickinson, "Macbeth had a claim to the throne which may well have been a double and better claim – perhaps going back through his mother to Kenneth II, as well as through his wife to Kenneth III". And according to *A Biographical Dictionary of Dark Age Britain: England, Scotland, Wales c.500 to c.1050*, "the subsequent marriage to Macbeth healed (the) dynastic war within Moray and united the houses of Moray and Kenneth III in mutual hostility to Malcolm II and his grandson Duncan". It is doubtful that Shakespeare knew much of the above – which is not to say he did not have knowledge outside the designated sources. It is not a convincing argument to say that what cannot be verified by reference to an extant written source must therefore be pure invention: there are other ways of acquiring knowledge – discussion with friends of work in progress, conversations in the pub, something overheard, etc. The authors of *A Biographical Dictionary* simply state that "Shakespeare's portrayal of Lady Macbeth as a ruthlessly ambitious woman who goaded her husband into slaying the innocent Duncan as he slept in Macbeth's castle has no historical foundation".

It is, though, of some significance that the play does not presume a commitment to the Law of Primogeniture (i.e. that the eldest son of a king automatically assumes the throne on the death of his father): Scottish monarchs were in all probability elected by clan chiefs. This arrangement is called tanistry, which the *Shorter OED* defines as "a system of life-tenure among the ancient Irish and Gaels, whereby the succession of an estate or dignity was conferred by election upon the 'eldest and worthiest' among the surviving kinsmen of a deceased lord." In actuality brawn was more of a deciding factor. There is a crucial moment in the play when policy – and Macbeth's hopes – are thwarted by Duncan's declaration:

> know
> We will establish our estate upon
> Our eldest, Malcolm, whom we name hereafter
> The Prince of Cumberland
>
> (Act I, scene 4, 37-40)

This, as we shall see later, is an important turning point in the drama.

History is, as we know, a construct, a fiction. Early Scottish history – we are told by Croft Dickinson – was invented by Hector Boece, a principal of Aberdeen University, between 1517 and 1525, and it is from him that "Shakespeare's tale of Macbeth, with the witches, Banquo, Macduff, and Birnam Wood" is ultimately derived. Shakespeare shaped the material he found in Holinshed, his direct source; he also added things not found there, such as the storm, the banqueting scene and Banquo's ghost.

3

Swelling Act

It is an exceptionally short play, the only one in the canon to conform to what, in *Romeo and Juliet,* is called "the two hours' traffic of our stage". *Hamlet*, the longest in performance, takes more than twice that amount of time. There are notorious textual problems for editors and speculations about 'lost' scenes or possible abridgements, prompting questions that will always remain stubbornly as questions: what does Lady Macbeth mean when she says "Nor time, nor place/ Did then adhere"? Was Cawdor secretly dealing with Norway? Does Banquo disturb Macbeth's sleep? Who is the third murderer? And then there is the question of additions – the Hecate scenes with their banal rhyming couplets, the two songs written by Middleton but, mercifully, jettisoned in modern production. This suggestion of interpolated scenes opens up speculation as to the authenticity of others – the scene in which the porter responds to the knocking at the gate, the perhaps over-long scene in England – and whether they represent a too-much relaxing of tension. And there are other irresolvable questions: because the play's setting is nocturnal (with all the symbolic overtones of that to be looked at later) was it more effectively performed at the indoor Blackfriars Theatre which the Company had acquired in 1608/9 and the Court? As the text of the play appears for the first time in the 1623 Folio, do we have copy from the Globe or from Blackfriars? Certain features of the play would be more plausibly done indoors – for example how the witches 'melt' into thin air. We know *Macbeth* was performed at the open-air Globe – an account of a 1611 production is given in the *Booke of Plaies* by the astrologer, Dr Simon Forman. It would appear that the simple carrying on of torches was sufficient to indicate night-time there.

So far we have looked at things that are mostly external to the play. It is now time we considered the play itself as a piece of drama – one with extraordinary poetic density, in which sensuous and intellectual experiences are vividly made palpable or, to use a word from modern technology, *virtual* – by poetry of the highest order. The approach will try to emulate the spirit of L.C. Knights in his book *Some Shakespearean Themes and an Approach to Hamlet* where he writes:

> Macbeth defines a particular kind of evil – the evil that results from a lust for power. The defining, as in all the tragedies, is in strictly poetic and dramatic terms. It is certainly not an abstract formulation, but lies rather in the drawing out of necessary consequences and implications of that lust both in the external and the spiritual worlds. Its meaning, therefore, is revealed in the expansion and unfolding of what lies within the initial evil, in terms of direct human experience. The logic is not formal but experiential, and demands from us, if we are to test its validity and feel its force, a fullness of imaginative response and a closeness of realization, in which both sensation and feeling become modes of understanding. Only when intellect, emotion, and a kind of direct sensory awareness work together can we enter fully in that exploratory and defining process.

But before doing this, it may be useful to briefly sketch in something of the history of criticism of the play and the kind of questions that have been posed in the process.

Is the play a Faustian drama of damnation, assuming/requiring an audience awareness of Christian perspectives? Is Macduff a St George to the dragon Macbeth in a battle of Good and Evil, a consequent re-establishing of order after disorder occasioned by sin and experienced cosmically? Is it a replaying of Adam and Eve in the Garden of Eden, the archetypal fall from Grace? Are there primitive folkloric patterns at work: winter darkness replaced by springtide regeneration, the march of green trees representing Nature's renewal? Are we to take the play as a history or a tragedy? As is the case in the history plays, the central subject of *Macbeth* is the rooting-out of treason and the reasserting of political hope. Is the purpose a moral one – fulfilling the Renaissance requirement of art to simultaneously delight and teach (tragedy seen as a warning against tyrants), something endorsed by Samuel Johnson when he tells us that in the play "The danger of ambition is well-described"? Is our interest primarily psychological – an inevitable interest in 'character' conditioned by two centuries of novel-reading and a hundred years of Freud? The supreme exemplar of this last approach – and someone still to be reckoned with ("his work on *Macbeth*," says Wain, "is as good as anything he ever did") – is A.C. Bradley, whose *Shakespearean Tragedy* was first published in 1904. So-called character-criticism was reacted against by L.C. Knights, heralding New Criticism, in his 1933 essay, *How Many Children Had Lady Macbeth?* and replaced by emphasis on analysing verbal textures, treating the plays as dramatic poems. The leading scholar in this approach was Caroline Spurgeon in her 1935 *Shakespeare's Imagery and What It Tells Us*. Historical studies have done much to provide useful handles to the play ... investigations of political, philosophical and religious perspectives. Books like E.M.W. Tillyard's *The Elizabethan World Picture* of 1943, though considered simplistic by some, still has interesting perspectives to offer. We have to be open-mindedly eclectic. As John Wain says "In studying a writer as many-sided as Shakespeare, a critic must take account of *everything*".

4

We Three

Coleridge has rightly said that "The true reason for the first appearance of the witches is to strike the keynote of the character of the whole drama". Shakespeare's contemporaries, as stated earlier, fully believed in the reality of witches, much as most of them believed in the existence of the Devil. They were not, as they are to us – to use Banquo's questioning word – "fantastical". Those of the play are Shakespeare's invention in as much as they are something different from what is suggested in Holinshed: they are a combination of those unfortunate women rooted out of villages throughout the realm, with their supposed 'familiars' (demons in animal form) and mythical figures (sybils, prophetesses) stretching back into pre-history – the title *Weird* Sisters allowing for this, making an explicit connection with Fate and Destiny – *wyrd* being the Anglo-Saxon word for Fate. It is interesting to note that, outside stage directions, the word "witch" appears only once in the text. Witches or weird sisters? The ambivalence is part of the dramatic effect. As Nicholas Brooke says: "Their ambiguity, of nature and of power, is fundamental to the ambiguities of experience and knowledge which the play develops".

They are associated with thunder and lightning and these – as with the storm reported later in Act II, scene 4 – show "the heavens, as troubled with man's act" (the battle). Or, to put it at its most simply obvious, there is something ominous abroad. How the witches enter and exit (do they really 'hover' in some way?) is left open but it is immediately clear (as so often with Shakespeare's opening scenes) that we are in the middle or at the tail-end of something: a discussion has already taken place. And here we have one of Coleridge's 'keynotes': the scene is a non-event; what takes place is discussion of a future event, a next meeting, a pointing forward to "the coming-on of time". This future meeting is to be a twilight one on a heath, after a battle, with someone called Macbeth. The words "will", "shall", "hereafter" (counterpointed by the even more pervasive appearance of "if", "would", "should") are part of the warp and woof of the play, as we will keep on seeing. The play, obsessed with futurity, is, to put it in a nutshell, about a man who believes he has forfeited his future, a "man forbid".

This opening twelve-line scene lasts no more than a couple of minutes but in it we are subjected to a syllabic hurly-burly (lines of 6/7/8/9 syllables), a ragbag of rhyming couplets. This ritualistic chanting ensures a willing suspension of disbelief into a supernatural dimension. It also perhaps embodies a distant echo of the hurly-burly going on somewhere else with its drums and the drumming hooves of horses.

As we have largely lost contact with the Elizabethan/Jacobean mode of thinking analogically, so we have lost (even more so) contact with number symbolism. This way of understanding persisted up and into the 18th century: a way of conceiving the universe as something highly structured, ordered mathematically (and therefore musically), that went back to Plato and Pythagoras, and was in the medieval and renaissance periods Christianised. Numbers were given symbolic life. They are, for instance, the secret language of early architecture. Three, four, seven, nine, twelve still have, if we think about them, residual significances today. Suffice to say for the moment, Shakespeare's audience would almost certainly have associated the three witches, parodically, with the Trinity, seen them therefore as intrinsically blasphemous, and shuddered at the thought of black masses. They were being allowed the vicarious thrill of the forbidden, a glimpse of evil agents (the Sisters are temptresses as well as prophetesses) ready at all times to subvert the natural order. Black birds – ravens, rooks, choughs – will hover over the play like witches' familiars.

In these opening whirlwind minutes we have the first mention of the word "done" – a word which is to ring like a death knell continually throughout the play. But more importantly the keynote of ambivalence (equivocation) is sounded in "lost and won", "Fair is foul, and foul is fair", and in the fog where the witches "hover". The importance of equivocation (making equations of opposites) has already been mentioned: it starts here and from now on will gather force to create a sticky web of antitheses and paradoxes. I am reminded of the oxymoronic way T.S. Fliot in *The Love Song of J. Alfred Prufrock* brings opposites together in such a way as to cancel each other out:

> There will be time to murder and create ...
>
> And for a hundred visions and revisions
> Before the taking of a toast and tea.

The witches leave the stage at the behest of their familiars, the cat Gray-Malkin and the toad Paddock; the third witch's "anon" suggesting 'here I come'. We expect to meet them again. Their "double, double, toil and trouble" will later be echoed in the description of the ferocity with which Macbeth and Banquo fought:

> As canons overcharg'd with double cracks;
> So they
> Doubly redoubled strokes upon the foe.
>
> (Act I, scene 2, 37-9)

and Lady Macbeth's welcoming words to Duncan:

> All our service
> In every point twice done and then done double.
>
> (Act I, scene 6, 14-15)

(It is worth noting that synonyms for treason are double-dealing and double-crossing).

Hilary Lloyd Yewlett in an internet essay on *Macbeth*, which claims that "Shakespearean criticism has been dominated by anglocentrism", offers an interesting perspective on the witches in suggesting their origins may be Celtic and asserting that Shakespeare "understood a great deal about Celtic customs and practices" and that he may have had knowledge of the medieval collection of Welsh tales, *The Mabinogion*. Whether we agree with this or not, some of her points are worth considering. Yewlett connects the witches with "prophetesses who assisted the Druids" and whose cauldron was a "prime female symbol ... the womb of the great goddess through which the dead could be reincarnated". This goddess has a "triple aspect" representing "three facets of womanhood", namely the maiden, the mother and the crone, and Yewlett points interestingly to the woodcut of the Weird Sisters in Holinshed which, though portraying them in Elizabethan dress, shows three ages represented – young, mature, old – with ravens (omens of death in Celtic mythology) flying above their heads. She also finds backing for this view in Terry Eagleton's *William Shakespeare*, where he describes them as "poets, prophetesses and devotees of female cult". Trevor Nunn's 1987 production of the play made use of this age-difference among the witches.

The cauldron, Yewlett goes on to say, was a sacred oblationary vessel, a source of wisdom, knowledge, inspiration and divination, a window into the Other World. Out of the cauldron in *Macbeth* we see Malcolm emerge carrying a tree (not only a pre-echo of the movement of Birnam Wood) but also, in Celtic mythology, associated with kingship: certain trees were sacred and symbolised "the king-becoming graces". Gods and goddesses metamorphosed themselves into animal forms. Yewlett finds the symbol of the boar in the reference to "killing swine" and links it to James' dismissal of his "Gaelic-speaking subjects as wolves and wild boars" as well as suggesting the possibility of implied anti-Catholic sentiment. In addition she has an interesting reading of "the pricking of my thumbs" which was a "specifically Scottish torment designed to test of the guilt or innocence of a witch by pricking the accused all over with a sharp instrument until the insensitive spot peculiar to a witch was found". Yewlett's view is that *Macbeth* "a play about ... a wild and Celtic realm 'civilised' by a 'legitimate' Scottish king with English sympathies, could not fail to please King James."

5

What Bloody Man is That?

Both *Othello* and *Macbeth* are filled with references to blood. In the former, blood is the sanguine humour; in *Macbeth*, however, the blood is physical. It stains the action; it smells and smokes; it gushes from wounds; gashes cry with it; Scotland itself, under the sway of Macbeth, is said to bleed; it is a part of the play's very palpable texture. The first human words in the text are "What bloody man is that?" asked of a captain come from the thick of battle to report a "bloody" Macbeth whose "brandished steel/ ... smoked bloody execution". In this scene the emphasis is on valour, which entails the spilling of blood.

Now we have to recognise that, in the eyes of most of Shakespeare's audience, the pursuit of honour on the battlefield was entirely praiseworthy. It is a key factor in *Othello*. And it is worth reminding ourselves of Antony in *Antony and Cleopatra* saying "If I lose mine honour,/ I lose myself" or Ventidius, in the same play, calling ambition "The soldier's virtue" ... especially when we remember Macbeth's claim that he only has "vaulting ambition to prick the sides of (his) intent" – an image of using spurs to make a horse jump. This is often interpreted as weakness: ambition as Macbeth's 'tragic flaw'. But he is not to be 'explained' so simplistically. Ambition is honourable. It is important to recognise that heroes live for posterity: how they are reported after their deaths is crucial; the force that drives them is the desire to enter the memory of the future. With this in mind, it is vital to observe the play Shakespeare makes of the conditional and future tenses in *Macbeth*.

A modern audience must inevitably pick up on an ambiguity: the description of Macbeth's strenuous feats of battle is not only an admiring account of soldierly prowess but also inescapably gruesome:

> ... brave Macbeth – well he deserves that name –
> Disdaining fortune, with his brandished steel
> Which smoked with bloody execution,
> Like valour's minion carved out his passage
> Till he faced the slave –
> Which ne'er shook hands nor bade to him farewell
> Till he unseamed him from the nave to the chops,
> And fixed his head upon our battlements.
>
> (Act I, scene 2, 16-23)

Our hero is, clearly, an unsqueamish man on the battlefield, one who may perhaps even relish his work as a butcher – an epithet applied to him at the end of the play. On the surface, though, this is praiseworthy behaviour and, in the pursuit of honour, deemed necessary and desirable features of a man's world. Suggestions that Macbeth's activities have an extra edge to them (a bonus for a modern audience) may simply be the product of sensibility different from that of Shakespeare's audience. The Globe after all was merely a few steps away from the bull- and bear-baiting pit and there is little need to remind ourselves of the barbarities of public executions of the time. It is worth noting that the last line of this passage contains an obvious irony, in that it is a pre-echo of what is to happen to Macbeth's detached head at the play's end.

Macbeth is about deeds and their human consequences. The deeds related in this scene are seen by those in it as honourable and are duly rewarded. Victory over the traitor has been achieved by two admirable soldiers: Banquo and Macbeth who were:

> As cannons overcharged with double cracks;
> So they
> Doubly redoubled strokes upon the foe.
> Except they meant to bathe in reeking wounds
> Or memorize another Golgotha
> I cannot tell –
>
> (Act I, scene 2, 37-42)

(we cannot escape noticing another textural pre-echo in the above speech – that of the witches' "double, double").

Hilary Lloyd Yewlett tells us that the "hurly-burly" of battle is "an apposite description of the way the Celts waged war ... rarely lengthy, for battles were often decided in no more than a few hours, usually "'ere set of sun". Celtic warriors, she avers, were known for their "formidable physical courage and reckless bravery". She also draws attention to how they often sought single combat.

Maintaining an awareness of the importance of tenses in the play (the conditional in particular – as I hope will become clearer later), we may note that this scene (Act I, scene 2) brings past events into the present by report and sets future events in motion. This occurs again and again throughout the play. It is, incidentally, also worth pointing out that one way Shakespeare has of signalling good men is to show them rewarding good news and loyalty in their fellows. Duncan is such a reward-giver. The key words in this scene are all commendatory: "worthy", "good", "hardy", "bloody", "valiant", "brave". Whether Shakespeare wishes us to pick up on suggestions of savagery is an open question.

The battle is concluded, has been lost and won, despite the fact that at one stage "Doubtful it stood" (ambivalence again); and the warrior, whose actions have been decisive and who later hopes to go along with chance, has been seen disdaining Fortune in the fray. The scene ends with Duncan's:

> No more that Thane of Cawdor shall deceive
> Our bosom interest. Go pronounce his present death,
> And with his former title greet Macbeth
> > (Act I, scene 2, 64-8)

and with the second mention of the ominous word "done" and the conclusive internally rhyming equation "What he hath lost, noble Macbeth hath won".

6

Light Thickens

Bradley describes *Macbeth* as "the most vehement, the most concentrated, perhaps we may say the most tremendous of the tragedies". If we allow "tremendous" its primary meaning of "such as to excite trembling, or awe" (*The Shorter OED*) there is nothing with which to quarrel. Leaving aside characterisation for the moment, *Macbeth* is a texturally extremely dense play, one in which the language plays a highly dynamic role, to the point of virtually being a physical assault on the audience. It is a play in which blood, darkness and evil are made almost tangible. The witches are manifestations, physical evidence of evil: they are 'there' because Macbeth, Banquo and the audience see them; they are also 'there' invisibly, hovering over the action in the form of portents, and in the way that evil is always 'there', whether we observe it or not. They are not there to determine the action (though everything they forecast ironically comes true) so much as to tempt Macbeth into hoping that what they prophesy will happen and so they create the context in which a fatal moment of choice is just too seductive. In fact, one may say that they are the *context* of the play, the outer layer of a multi-layered dramatic experience. And if the play is a nightmare, which paradoxically Macbeth (the Glamis who "hath murdered sleep", the Macbeth who "shall sleep no more") and the audience experience *awake and in daylight*, then we may thank the witches for turning the key in the door of their and our collective unconscious or, in Shakespeare's phrase, our "imaginary forces". As echoes and reminders of the witches, ominous and portentous birds hover over the action: the screech-owl that prophesies death, black crows, choughs, ravens. Horses are frequently mentioned or implied – most decisively in the nightmarish storm during which Duncan's bolt out of their stables, turn wild and begin eating each other – in psychological terms, act regressively (wild horses in dreams often symbolise the uncontrollable instinctive forces that may erupt from the unconscious). Evil spirits are invoked; murderers glide obsequiously into action; unprepossessing items are stirred into a cauldron out of which a grim pageant emerges; the storm itself that sets nature at odds with itself:

> Thou seest the heavens, as troubled with man's act,
> Threatens his bloody stage. By the clock 'tis day,
> And yet dark night strangles the travelling lamp;
> Is't night's predominance or the day's shame
> That darkness does the face of earth entomb
> When living life should kiss it?
>
> (Act II, scene 4, 5-10)

This is a storm in which the "earth was feverous and did shake", in which (in a perfect analogue of Macbeth's killing of Duncan) a "falcon towering in her pride of place/ Was by a mousing owl hawked at, and killed."

Evil and darkness are, of course, indissolubly linked: one of the Devil's titles is the Prince of Darkness. It may be of some significance that Macbeth's servant is called Seyton, the pronunciation of which name the audience must hear as Satan. The play is set in darkness (or rather darkness with a confusion of torches) and in appropriately climatic conditions for evil – storm, thunder, lightning, rain, fog and filthy air. The witches are a confused mixture of the elements; they are seen by Banquo as composed of water bubbling out of earth, which is, according to the doctrine of the humours, associated with melancholy, the colour black and the quality of coldness:

> The earth hath bubbles as the water has,
> And these are of them. Whither are they vanished?
>
> (Act I, scene 3, 78-9)

More likely intended, though, is the phlegmatic humour (cold/ moist) traditionally associated with women (hence tearfulness!), old age, Winter, the West Wind.

Macbeth's immediate reply is:

Into the air; and what seemed corporal
Melted, as breath into the wind.

(It would be interesting to know how in the Globe theatre this vanishing by melting might have taken place). The melancholy humour (or black bile) is also associated with the lower body, the zodiacal signs of Libra, Scorpio ("O, full of scorpions is my mind, dear wife" – Scorpio was, incidentally, associated with the genitals) and Sagittarius. Other connections were with density ("light thickens"), maturity, Autumn ("my way of life is fallen into the sere") and the North Wind. It is clear that the witches have power over the winds:

Second Witch:	I'll give thee a wind.
First Witch:	Th' art kind.
Third Witch:	And I another.

(Act I, scene 3, 11-13)

(In Act IV, scene 1, Macbeth acknowledges this power when he says "Though you untie the winds and let them fight/ Against the churches.")

The witches' reappearance in this third scene of the play is rendered in irregular and disorderly syllabic lines, which by the first witch's third utterance, settle into the incantatory playground seven-syllable line. In a gross parody of the previous scene, past events are recounted and here gloated over before shifting gear into the future tense:

But in a sieve I'll thither sail
And like a rat without a tail
I'll do, I'll do, and I'll do.

(Act I, scene 3, 8-10)

We have already mentioned that "done" is a word that drums away throughout the play: we are also made aware of "do", "doing", "did", "deed". Deeds and their consequences are what the play is about. In the earlier *Julius Caesar*, Brutus, unable to sleep, talks of " … some worthy cause to wish/ Things done, undone."

Among other motifs weaving their way through the play (and there will be others mentioned as we go along) is that of sleep/

sleeplessness. The master o'th' *Tiger* is being cursed to the point at which he will "dwindle, peak, and pine", the process initiated by robbing him of sleep:

> Sleep shall neither night nor day
> Hang upon his penthouse lid.
> He shall live a man forbid.

(Act I, scene 3, 19-21)

Not only is this the future intruding on the present, it is also a forecast of what will eventually happen to Macbeth's own state of mind.

7

King Hereafter

Macbeth's famous first words constitute a seeming paradox: "So foul and fair a day I have not seen" – "foul" the weather, "fair" the victory. What ensues in this meeting with the witches is a continuous linguistic tipping up and down of scales in the weighing of the seeds of time:

> ... which grain will grow and which will not,
>
> Your favours nor your hate
>
> Lesser than Macbeth, and greater
>
> Not so happy, yet much happier
>
> Thou shalt get kings, though thou be none.

We are dealing in futures, in what occurs 'hereafter' (another word that will resonate throughout the play, drastically so in Macbeth's reaction to the news of his wife's death) In this scene we can say that, through prediction, the future plays cruelly with the present. The future tense is used throughout. The witches do not stay to be interrogated as to why they offer "such prophetic greeting."

The confusion of the elements they are composed of and represent is extended to the question of the witches' gender. Banquo is bewildered:

> You should be women,
> And yet your beards forbid me to interpret
> That you are so.
>
> (Act I, scene 3, 44-6)

Are they female, male, or androgynous?

Laying choppy fingers on skinny lips suggests that they have no wish to speak to Banquo first. It is clearly Macbeth, as the first scene of the play has already told us, who is their primary target.

But it is Banquo who does most of the talking. At first he seems – perhaps because of the system of tanistry – unfazed by the predictions made – which he describes as "Of noble having, and of royal hope" – on behalf of Macbeth. What does strike him, however, is the manner of Macbeth's reaction:

> Good sir, why do you start, and seem to fear
> Things that do sound so fair?
>
> (Act I, scene 3, 50-1)

noticing how his "noble partner … seems rapt withal." When Macbeth eventually puts his reaction in words, it is – as if his conscience is already marshalling counter-arguments – one of seeming incredulity:

> By Sinell's death I know I am Thane of Glamis;
> But how of Cawdor? The Thane of Cawdor lives
> A prosperous gentleman. And to be king
> Stands not within the prospect of belief –
> No more than to be Cawdor.
>
> (Act I, scene 3, 70-4)

Conscience and "thinking too precisely on th' event", as Hamlet says (and Lady Macbeth knows), makes cowards of us all. *Macbeth* is a play about the workings of conscience.

When the predictions start to look as though they might come about, Banquo's reaction is: "What, can the devil speak true?" He is less tempted, more fearful, suspicious of what he calls "the instruments of darkness", whereas Macbeth, though still uncertain (is he the ditherer his wife says he is?) sees the predictions as transformed to "truths" and as "happy prologues to the swelling act/ Of the imperial theme." Again, we witness a tipping up and down of scales.

Banquo's wish to discuss the matter is put off, deferred (as it is on further occasions) by Macbeth's aside. This puts him into what I will call *if*-mode: from now on the future tense starts to be overtaken by the conditional: "if"/"would" /"could" /"should" begin to weave their pattern into the texture of the play.

As if to still his disquietude, the man who once disdained Fortune now adopts a *che sarà sarà* (What will be, will be) attitude:

> If chance will have me king, why chance may crown me
> Without my stir.
>
> (Act I, scene 3, 144-5)

but not before he has revealed to us why he is so "rapt":

> Present fears
> Are less than horrible imaginings.
> My thought, whose murder yet is but fantastical,
> Shakes so my single state of man
> That function is smothered in surmise,
> And nothing is but what is not.
>
> (Act I, scene 3, 136-141)

In other words, he is *imagining the possibility* of murdering Duncan. This does not necessarily indicate, as some critics insist, a predetermined intention to do so. In fact he is recoiling from what may have been an involuntary image momentarily flashed into his mind. What is clear is that Macbeth has already begun his sojourn in the mind-torturing world of *if*, become subject to what medieval writers called the agenbite of inwit.

Macbeth of course does not know that Duncan, in the next scene, is to put an obstacle in his way, publicly announcing and therefore projecting a different future:

> know
> We will establish our estate upon
> Our eldest, Malcolm, whom we name hereafter
> The Prince of Cumberland:
>
> (Act I, scene 4, 37-40)

Macbeth is forced to realise he can no longer rely on chance, on things happening in the course of nature, but must act if he is to attain his desire, must plunge into the world of sin. From this moment the witches own his soul. He makes a decision – and as a consequence becomes, from this moment on, irretrievably, humanly responsible for his actions. Individual choice and freewill are now in play: Macbeth has *chosen* to forfeit his future. As Jan Kott in his influential book, *Shakespeare Our Contemporary*, has written: "In *Macbeth* history, as well as crime, has been shown through personal experience. It is a matter of decision, choice and compulsion".

And yet, all that the witches prophesy does actually come true. The questions to be asked are: would everything have come true without Macbeth's stir anyway and, most difficult of all, was his choice to do the deed as pre-ordained as the other events? It is like asking if Judas was part of God's plan and, if so, what kind of divine justice that might represent. All we can say is that human beings resent the idea that everything is pre-determined, that free will and human choice are cruel illusions.

8

Bellona

We have the measure of Macbeth as a brave soldier, as someone considered admirable by his peers. Yet the play explores – as with so many other plays of the period – what happens when a tried and tested soldier, released from battle, discovers himself in a domestic setting, one in which he may find himself uncomfortable. In a newspaper interview (*The Times,* 17th February 2003) the actor, Sir Ian McKellen, is quoted as saying "Shakespeare's soldiers can be trusted … as long as they are soldiering, but they make dreadful politicians and they are hopeless in their private lives." Peacetime is a breeding place for villainy and messed-up lives. The Devil has work for idle hands.

In the case of Macbeth, as Jan Kott has said, "He can become a King, so he must become a King." To be King becomes a cause, a *raison d'être* – in which he ironically and paradoxically loses his *raison d'être*, his life ending up as "Signifying nothing". Lady Macbeth, receiving her husband's letter, determines to set in motion the Machiavellian scheming, already gnawing away at his sense of right and wrong, which will lead to both their deaths. And she will put a kind of emotional pressure on him that he will find impossible to withstand.

If one were to ask which of the two is the stronger character, Macbeth or Lady Macbeth, the spontaneous answer will probably say that she is. She certainly gives the impression, when we first meet her, of being a formidable character – in the context of the history of drama, we often find her aligned with powerful female characters like Clytemnestra and Medea. She knows her husband inside out and gives quite a different account of him from what we have so far been exposed to: he is "too full of the milk of human kindness/ To catch the nearest way." ("Kindness" means not only compassion and gentleness but common humanity or what is considered natural in a human being, whilst *her* emphasis is consistently on things unnatural). In other words, she distrusts his feminine side. Her reaction to the letter (in which the past enters the present, though largely concerned with the future) starts with the present tense "art", moves rapidly into "shalt be", then includes a bombardment of conditionals ("wouldst" used six times): she knows he's an *if*-man.

She also has a penchant for grim puns:

> Thou wouldst be great,
> Art not without ambition, but without
> The illness should attend it. What thou wouldst highly
> That wouldst thou holily …
>
> (Act I, scene 5, 15-18)

(Later she will utter one of the grimmest puns in English literature when she says, "I'll gild the faces of the grooms withal/ For it must seem their guilt.")

Her word "illness" (the motif of disease also runs right through the play) carries, as well as connotations of sickness, the idea of evil (bad-ness) and sin. In other words, her view of her husband is that he has a too-scrupulous conscience, he is a ditherer, and needs a good talking-to:

> Hie thee hither
> That I may pour my spirits in thine ear,
> And chastise with the valour of my tongue
> All that impedes thee from the golden round
> Which fate and metaphysical aid doth seem
> To have thee crowned withal.
>
> (Act I, scene 5, 23-8)

She uses the word "chastise" as if intending to treat him, on his return, like a wayward child (does the word contain suggestions of rough sex?) and she appropriates the masculine word "valour". This assumption of masculinity is found again on her receiving news of Duncan's intended visit when she utters the words "Under *my* battlements" (my italics), which she will significantly alter later, with the announcement of Duncan's murder, to "What in our house?"

Her invocation of the "spirits/ That tend on mortal thoughts" has in it the express desire to eradicate the qualities belonging to the 'weaker sex'. The speech is highly charged sexually: she wishes to "Stop up th' access and passage to remorse", to turn the milk of her "woman's breasts" to gall; above all, she wishes for "no compunctious visitings of nature." The surface meaning is that she desires to remove from her nature all signs of what she understands to be female/ feminine, but one cannot help detecting a sub-surface of something unpleasantly, obscenely gynaecological. Does she, like Ibsen's Hedda Gabler, loathe her own feminine nature or is she energised by sexual frustration? (We may wish to notice here the implied theme of progeny, another vivid thread woven into the texture of the play). This dedication to evil ends with the suggestion that she herself will be the murderer:

> Come, thick night,
> And pall thee in the dunnest smoke of hell,
> That my keen knife see not the wound it makes,
> Nor heaven peep through the blanket of the dark
> To cry, 'Hold, hold!'
>
> (Act I, scene 5, 48-52)

The question to be asked (in view of her later appearances in the play) is how far we take this as literal? Is this a formidably strong character, a truly evil woman, beyond the pale, determined to be Queen, or is her speech mere bravado, revving herself up for the scornful persuasions she is to bring to bear on her husband? Do the sentiments proceed out of a "heat-oppressèd brain"? Is she, to put it bluntly, all talk?

In *Antony and Cleopatra* Agrippa tells us that the gods "give us … faults to make us men." In other words, it is our weaknesses and how we manage them that mark us out as human. Indecisiveness (more so than it is with Hamlet) is the mark of Macbeth, coupled with gullibility (more so than is the case with Othello). These lead him into the sleepless world in which clocks can never be turned back and time itself becomes meaningless. The world as a waking nightmare.

Lady Macbeth later becomes a walking, literal nightmare. Sleep in her case is not the sleep:

> ... that knits up the ravelled sleave of care,
> The death of each day's life, sore labour's bath,
> Balm of hurt minds, great nature's second course,
> Chief nourisher in life's feast.
>
> (Act II, scene 2, 35-8)

Her tortured sleep-walking is in ironic counterpoint to his sleepless nightmare existence. In both their cases the past haunts the present and cancels the future. It is worth noting the words she uses when he appears before her for the first time:

> Great Glamis, worthy Cawdor!
> Greater than both by the all-hail hereafter!
> Thy letters have transported me beyond
> This ignorant present, and I feel now
> The future in the instant.
>
> (Act I, scene 5, 52-6)

The future in the instant: she too is "rapt". Yet despite her declared intention to murder ("my keen knife"), Lady Macbeth is an organiser, not a doer:

> He that's coming
> Must be provided for; and you shall put
> This night's great business into my dispatch,
> Which shall to all our nights and days to come
> Give solely sovereign sway and masterdom.
>
> (Act I, scene 5, 64-8)

(We cannot fail to register yet another sinister pun in the phrase "provided for" and note the masculine word "masterdom"). Tingling with (sexual?) expectation, she eagerly spurs him into action, to chastise him with the valour of her tongue and make him reach out for what is implied in the word "hereafter" ("What thou art promised"). She forces him to encounter a future she herself is greedy to possess. All that is needed is not to admit fear:

> Only look up clear:
> To alter favour ever is to fear.

(Act I, scene 5, 69-70)

She is the one who does the preparatory work:

> his two chamberlains
> Will I with wine and wassail so convince
> That memory, the warder of the brain,
> Shall be a fume ...

(Act I, scene 7, 63-6)

and, with Macbeth in a panic after the event, the tidying-up:

> Give me the daggers. The sleeping and the dead,
> Are but as pictures. 'Tis the eye of childhood
> That fears a painted devil. If he do bleed,
> I'll gild the faces of the grooms withal,
> For it must seem their guilt.

(Act II, scene 2, 53-7)

She is the resolute one: all *he* says in the first of these scenes (as he already has done and will do again with Banquo) is "We will speak further." And yet for all her determination, he is the one to do the deed; and she is the one who cracks first; the one to make the telling admission "Had he not resembled/ My father as he slept, I had done't"; who says, in her sleep-walking, "Yet who would have thought the old man to have had so much blood in him". Both these remarks (and perhaps the confession that she had fortified her nerves with drink – "That which hath made them drunk, hath made me bold") expose a vulnerability and suggest that, for all her assumption of masculine characteristics, she too, like her husband is a coward. Or, to put it more positively, that she too, beneath her Bellona's armour, has a conscience, a sense of right and wrong. The renunciation she makes of her womanhood may be seen as a tactical ploy. Is she really as "superficial and shallow" as Wain proposes?

Lady Macbeth, if we are to believe Yewlett, is in the tradition of the "mighty female rulers of the ancient British world – a match for any warrior king". She aligns her, not with Medea and Clytemnestra, but with the Queens Mebh, Cartimandura, and Boudicca. There are,

33

however, contrasts within the play we cannot ignore. Lady Macbeth herself recognises and admits the feminine side of her nature in her desire to repress it; she also recognises the feminine side of her husband's nature in wanting to chastise it. Shakespeare may be said to be expressing the conventional view of women as the 'weaker sex' by showing her will as having collapsed in the sleep-walking scene. It is she who now proclaims "What's done cannot be undone."

But there are other women in the play. The "womanly" Lady Macduff, left bewildered and defenceless, deals lovingly with and gently teases her young son, puts up a "womanly defence" of innocence, and bravely confronts her murderers. (Her fate and that of her son raise the question we will pick up on later: how in all justice we understand the deaths of the innocent). Also mentioned is Duncan's wife, a paragon of piety and selflessness. Macduff tells Malcolm that his mother:

> the queen that bore thee,
> Oftener upon her knees than on her feet,
> Died every day she lived.
>
> (Act IV, scene 3, 109-11)

And it is important to note that the sacral value placed on Malcolm's virginity:

> I am yet
> Unknown to woman, never was forsworn,
> Scarcely have coveted what was mine own,
> At no time broke my faith, would not betray
> The devil to his fellow, and delight
> No less in truth than life.
>
> (Act IV, scene 3, 125-130)

Virginity is, like cleanliness, next to God. It denotes purity in a society whose religion thought celibacy the highest of virtues and sex permitted only in marriage for the purposes of procreation. If celibacy was not possible then chastity, with its insistence on fidelity, was the next best thing. Lechery was one of the Seven Deadly Sins.

It has to be said that this betrayal of the feminine side of Lady Macbeth's nature, outside her sleep-walking, is only available in the comment about Duncan's resemblance to her father; that in the sleepwalking scene it is the audience and not Lady Macbeth herself who is conscious of the exposure of her guilt; and, finally, that if, as is suggested at the end of the play, she takes her own life, this may be understood by most of Shakespeare's audience to be a guarantee of a place in hell.

9

The Sticking Place

Shakespeare's audience had behind them three-quarters of a century of monarchical concern with procreation and anxiety over miscarriages, childlessness (in the case of the Virgin Queen) and succession. The Tudor dynasty had provided England with a king who needed six wives and the mighty upheaval of the Reformation to produce heirs. Each one of them, in their way, like their father, created political and religious havoc. Edward VI, during his short life, was a puritanical zealot, attempting to strengthen anti-papacy politics and the Anglican Church far more rigidly than his father. His sister, Mary (Bloody Mary), then succeeded him, savagely restoring the Roman Catholic religion and conducting a reign of terror. Following her, Elizabeth I came to the throne renewing Anglicanism in a moderate form and, relatively speaking, stabilising the business of England. She died childless in 1603.

In his introduction to the *Oxford Shakespeare*, Nicholas Brooke argues that "no play of Shakespeare's makes so little allusion to sex ...Where sexuality might most be expected, between the Macbeths, or in the Weird Sisters' obscenities, it is completely absent." Jan Kott on the other hand has argued that "These two are sexually obsessed with each other, and yet have suffered a great erotic defeat." (Sexual tension certainly gave an edge to a celebrated production in 1955 featuring Laurence Olivier and Vivien Leigh, staged during a turbulent period in their marriage: the theatre-critic, Kenneth Tynan, who had originally panned it, later revised his opinion, telling John Russell Taylor that "the combination of Olivier and Vivien, with its emphasis on the way Macbeth is held in sexual thrall by his lady and so will do anything to please her, made more sense of the play than any he had seen").Harold Bloom, in *Shakespeare: the Invention of the Human*, goes as far as to say that the Macbeths "are profoundly in love with each other. Indeed, with unsurpassing irony Shakespeare presents them as the happiest married couple in all his work." "Happiest" is hardly the word but certainly it is a marriage in which sexual blackmail plays an important role. And how can one escape noticing the extent to which the play is filled with references to procreation? And to its opposite in words like "fruitless", "barren", or the image of miscarriage in "birth-strangled babe, ditch-delivered by a drab", or in the cruel joke of Macduff being "from his mother's womb untimely ripp'd", and such mention as "the milk of human kindness", "the sweet milk of concord", "the babe that milks me", not forgetting the "pendant bed and procreant bed" of the house martin built where the air "smells wooingly".

Whether Shakespeare knew that Gruoch, the historical Lady Macbeth, had been previously married to Gillacogmain and had a son by him called Lulach, is impossible to prove and perhaps foolish of us to imagine, but it would make sense (given that the Macbeths have no children) of her otherwise unaccountable remark "I have given suck, and know/ How tender 'tis to love the babe that milks me." And it would provide backing for the way she seems to play upon male anxieties about sexuality:

> From this time
> Such I account thy love. Art thou afeard
> To be the same in thine own act and valour
> As thou art in desire?
>
> (Act I, scene 7, 38-41

– later echoed in the Porter's references to sexual performance in Act II, scene 3. But the operative word in the above lines is "love". "Such I account thy *love*", not courage or valour. It is also worth noting her words "their fitness now/ Does unmake you" – "make" is another version of mate or sexual partner. Her unsexing of herself gains a sinister correlative in her word "unmake". The word "desire" is also full of suggestion, especially when coupled in her speech with "act and valour". And it is interesting that she injects the word "dare" into the situation: "dare" as a necessary leap from present to future.

Given her penchant for puns and double-meanings, it is not going too far, I feel, to understand a sexual sub-text in the word "desire". We know that this marriage is childless or, to put it another way, has yet to prove itself with a natural outcome in children. This is not to leave out the possibility, as John Wain suggests, that the Macbeths "may have had children at some time or another, but as we see them in the play they are lost to any such creative purpose; they stand against life" – though I must confess that this sounds to me like a critic working to a formula in which the equation is Life and Anti-life, Creative and Destructive. It is not, I think, as simple as this.

I have already drawn attention to the obsessive strand of imagery in the play taken from things associated with progeny and babyhood; and it is important to remember key features of the plot too depend on it – Banquo's children, Macduff's children, and Macduff's caesarean delivery. Bloom has this to say:

> The terror that we experience, as audience or as readers, when we suffer *Macbeth* seems to me, in many ways, sexual in nature, if only because murder increasingly becomes a mode of sexual expression. Unable to beget children, Macbeth slaughters them.

It is a well-known fact that death and sex were inextricably and punningly linked in the Elizabethan/Jacobean mind; and there was the belief that human will was required to obey reason rather than passion; the emotions were to be kept in order by reason. Reason was the quality shared with the angels. This helped human beings to aspire Heavenwards, whereas passion, shared with the beasts, if not properly regulated, tempted the soul downwards to hell. And it is worth remembering that the Elizabethan/Jacobean sensibility, without the benefit of Freud, perhaps had small notion of a subconscious mind, at least as we know it: dreams and fantasies were popularly thought to come either from heaven or from hell.

What Lady Macbeth leans on is her husband's sense of himself as a man ("When you durst do it, then you were a man".) Like the witches with their predictions (which she takes as promises), she too implies a promise when she speaks of "all our days *and nights* to come." (In a television programme about the painter Titian, I was struck by a comment on his paintings of nudes and their erotic impact on patrons that commissioned them, to the effect that the more the patron was aroused the better the chance of producing children).

Now we know Macbeth is a nonpareil in the masculine arena of battle, has nothing to prove there. It is no wonder then that his reaction to the above speech is a ratty:

> Prithee peace.
> I dare do all that may become a man;
> Who dares do more is none.
>
> (Act I, scene 7, 45-7)

This is the soldier and the thane replying ... but she is also, at a deeper level, addressing Macbeth the husband, in other words demanding that he prove he is a man to *her.* Could it be, in the words of Kott, that "She demands murder from Macbeth as a confirmation of his manhood, almost as an act of love" – which is perhaps tantamount to saying he's on a promise? He for his part – if we allow for knowledge of second marriage – may be said to carry in his head the corrosive anxiety that sexual comparisons are being unsettlingly hinted at. Her playing the man's part is provocative and her knowledge of male sexual anxiety may well be the product of other relationships or of a canny observation of men, and Macbeth in particular. The twist of the knife comes in her declaration that she'd be prepared to kill her own child "had I so sworn/ As you have done to this." (There is no evidence that he has sworn anything). In other words she would destroy in herself all trace of that which makes her a woman. It is a threat to "Stop up 'the access and passage to remorse'"; and if she denies that in herself, an inference for him would be that she would be denying something to him too. It is no wonder that he gives in to her persuasions and declares:

> Bring forth men-children only!
> For thy undaunted mettle should compose
> Nothing but males.
>
> (Act I, scene 7, 72-4)

The threat has been lifted: all he has to do is screw his courage to the sticking place (I am not convinced by footnotes telling us that this is a reference to crossbows or the tuning of musical instruments) for continued sexual relations to be guaranteed. The threat proves itself to be a form of stimulation in disguise. Freudians would doubtless see the dagger and the sword that kills Duncan as phallic.

I confess that some of what I've been saying is based on surmise, rooted in intuition; and I admit that a sexless (or unsexed) Lady Macbeth is feasible ... she could be seen for example, in a play built of antitheses, as the bad angel of medieval drama arguing against the good angel of her husband's conscience. I, for one, would need to be convinced, however, that a production not acknowledging this had not sacrificed a most plausible dynamic. For one thing, there would be no point in assassinating Banquo and attempting the killing of his son, Fleance, if Macbeth didn't believe that he could eventually father children and therefore a line of kings. For heroes, posterity also means the genetic continuation of a dynasty through the male line. "Bring forth men-children only," he tells his wife. There is a sense in which Lady Macbeth becomes a fourth witch or has absorbed, through her invocation of the "murdering ministers", the characteristics of the three originals.

10

Fatal Entrance

In Act IV, scene 3, Macduff tells Malcolm that his late father was "a most sainted king" and most productions of the play bring on a Duncan dressed in white to emphasise, like the milk-white horse in early cowboy films, the presence of a good guy. As with the other characters – outside the two main ones – he is not deeply characterised. We have already noticed that he is a reward-giver; he is also an inspirer of loyalty ("Your highness'part, is to receive our duties") and a respecter of reputation and deserving. Just after the beginning of the play, a man whose "gashes cry for help" defers help in order to bring heartening news to his King, a king who takes up arms against traitors and is decisive in his dealings with them. The traitor Cawdor is summarily dispatched – though not without some irony, in that he:

> set forth
> A deep repentance. Nothing in his life
> Became him like the leaving it.
>
> (Act I, scene 4, 7-9)

which prompts Duncan to admit:

> There's no art
> To find the mind's construction in the face.
> He was a gentleman on whom I built
> An absolute trust.
>
> (Act I, scene 4, 12-15)

These comments, applied retrospectively to Macbeth, whom he considers a "peerless kinsman", carry a cargo of irony, as does Macbeth's statement:

> I'll be myself the harbinger and make joyful
> The hearing of my wife with your approach;
>
> > (Act I, scene 4, 46-7)

"Joyful" is the word!

The emphasis, once the hurly-burly's done, is on love and, in particular, growth. Duncan tells Macbeth:

> I have begun to plant thee, and will labour
> To make thee full of growing.
>
> > (Act I, scene 4, 29-30)

Banquo responds to Duncan's "let me enfold thee,/ And hold thee to my heart" with the words:

> > There if I grow,
> The harvest is your own.
>
> > (Act I, scene 4, 33-4)

But, unwittingly, Duncan complicates matters by nominating his eldest son, Malcolm, as his heir, and if we understand kingship as being an elective process among the Scots this announcement is a pivotal moment for Macbeth. He cannot now rely on chance but has to act:

> The Prince of Cumberland! That is a step
> On which I must fall down, or else o'erleap,
> For in my way it lies. Stars, hide your fires,
> Let not light see my black and deep desires.
>
> > (Act I, scene 4, 49-52)

Lady Macbeth is clearly taken by surprise on receiving the news that Duncan is to visit "my battlements": she tells the messenger "Thou 'rt mad to say it" but she can scarcely contain her excitement. The murder of Duncan is already, in her mind, as good as performed, and she makes that quite plain to her husband on his arrival home. He informs her that "Duncan comes here tonight" then, in answer to her "And when goes hence?", simply replies "Tomorrow, as he purposes". We cannot escape noticing all this language denoting future events nor Macbeth's unthinking answer, on which she pounces:

O never

Shall sun that morrow see!

(Act I, scene 5, 59-60)

The sun is of course a symbol of royalty. Whatever her motives, the decisiveness and the excitement are inescapable. Is this the bored housewife with the opportunity to see some action, self-assertively spice up her life, her neglected emotions? If Shakespeare had knowledge of the Macbeths' history outside his principal source, he might even have supposed she was fired up with political motives. Croft Dickinson tells us:

> ... Boite had also a daughter, Gruoch, who had married first Gillacogmain, mormaer of Moray, and, secondly, Macbeth, whose father, Findlaech, had been mormaer of Moray, and who was Gillacogmain's cousin. These mormaers of Moray were largely independent of the Scottish king – an independence helped by the barrier of the Mounth; the Irish annalists accord them the title of *ri*, or 'king'; they could claim to be, and perhaps were, kings in their own right; and there was certainly an old feud between them and Malcolm II. Moreover, in Gruoch's two marriages there lay a definite danger that the 'House of Moray' might rule all Scotland, both north and south, unless Malcolm could secure the accession to the throne of Duncan, who could, through his mother's marriage to Crinan, abbot of Dunkeld, count on the support of Atholl against Moray.

The main point in all this convoluted history is that the historical Macbeth, as pointed out earlier, had a better claim to the throne than Duncan, whom he in fact killed:

> near Elgin, in the Moray country (where doubtless Duncan was seeking to remove his rival), and thereby succeeded to the throne. All 'in manner of the Scots', but made to appear wild and strange by Hector Boece, and thence made famous by Shakespeare.

In Act I, scene 6, Duncan appears before Macbeth's castle. The stage directions in the Folio edition ask for hautboys and torches. This indicates that, though the conversation between the King and Banquo suggests daytime, the scene is nocturnal. The talk is of fresh air (in contrast to the fog and filthy air of the heath) and the "temple-haunting martlet" (in contrast to the black birds that appear in the imagery of the rest of the play). The martlet (or house-martin) confers a benediction on the castle. The religious overtones are obvious: it is a temple-haunting bird, in a place where "heaven's breath/ Smells wooingly". It is here it hangs its "pendant bed and procreant cradle". Purity of air, benediction, domestic love ("wooingly") and procreation are all poetically interwoven and potent with irony: Inverness Castle is no temple but the place Duncan is to make a fatal entrance under Lady Macbeth's battlements, whose gates are later likened to the gates of hell.

She and Duncan exchange formal courtesies. One of her lines stays echoing in our minds when she declares:

> All our service
> In every point twice done and then done double
> Were poor and single business ...
> (Act I, scene 6, 14-16)

Here, again, is that fatal word "done", coupled with the witches' word "double", ostensibly innocent words redolent with sinister undercurrents. ("Double" of course ties in with the ambiguities, the equivocations of which the play is constructed, as is made distinctly clear in Macbeth's comment in Act V, scene 6, about "these juggling fiends" that "palter with us in a double sense.") At the beginning of the next scene Macbeth is to bang the drum with the word "done" three times in two lines, playing on at least two meanings: the completion of an action but also the wishful thinking ("if") that an action, once completed, might be totally voided of consequence. Nicholas Brooke draws attention to the proverb "the thing done is not to do." More significantly, R.W. Holder's *The Faber Dictionary of Euphemisms* tells us the Elizabethans, like us, used the verb to do to mean to have sex with, citing Ben Jonson's "Doing a filthy pleasure is, and short". Brooke ignores this and much more in his assertion that the play has so little allusion to sex.

It is an obvious matter to say that Macbeth has a heated imagination; what is not so often remarked on is that his mind has a metaphysical bent and tends to oscillate between the thought *if-only* and the counter-thought *yes-but*, and often, in the process, becomes paralysed by their irreconcilability. Like George Herbert's picture of Man in his poem *Affliction IV*, he is:

A wonder tortured in the space
Betwixt this world and that of grace.

a walking paradox, tormented by the agenbite of inwit, by what he himself calls "judgement". The imagery of his soliloquy is drawn mainly from horse-riding and, in a manner that can only be termed visionary, is further associated with babies and cherubim. In his mind the future has become perilous: he puts himself on the rack of "if", the conditionals, "should", "could", and the subjunctive "were" and "might be". He is arguing with himself "against the deed".

Macbeth's attitude to his proposed victim at this point reinforces the simple characterisation we have been outlining. Duncan:

Hath borne his faculties so meek, hath been
So clear in his great office, that his virtues
Will plead like angels, trumpet-tongued against
The deep damnation of his taking-off.
(Act I, scene 7, 17-20)

We can almost believe that Duncan fulfils the "king-becoming graces" listed by Malcolm in Act IV:

… justice, verity, temperance, stableness,
Bounty, perseverance, mercy, lowliness,
Devotion, patience, courage, fortitude.
(Act IV, scene 3, 92-4

– qualities that Macbeth, when king, will be seen (with the possible exceptions of the last two) to be wanting. But we may well imagine them operating in Duncan. We may also suppose that Macbeth, in Act I, scene 7, implicitly understands them as proper attributes of kingship and therefore knows what he is depriving Scotland of in killing its king.

Duncan is present in Macbeth's mind as his king, an honoured guest, and his relative: he is also an integral element in Macbeth's own reputation (which Cassio in *Othello* calls "the immortal part of myself", the loss of which represents a descent into the bestial). At this point in the play, Macbeth's arguments "against the deed" are winning through. He tells his wife "We will proceed no further in this business". It is now up to her to make him change his mind.

She does so by the means I have suggested, at the same time interweaving in her persuasions the words "do", "done", "would", "shall", "will" and references to babies, sleep and drunkenness – the last two of these, metaphorically, forms of death – as is sex (the porter associates drinking with lechery – ambivalently so, in that it "provokes and unprovokes".)

11

False Face

From now on, in more ways than one, she and her husband will "mock the time" and hide "the false heart" by wearing a "false face". They will dress themselves in "borrowed robes".

The first person to be presented with "false face" is Banquo. He simply declares himself to be a man of integrity. When Macbeth promises that he will talk with Banquo further about the Weird Sisters, he tells him "It shall make honour for you" and receives the reply:

> So I lose none
> In seeking to augment it, but still keep
> My bosom franchised, and allegiance clear,
> I shall be counselled.
>
> (Act II, scene 1, 26-9)

In other words, he will speak with Macbeth on condition that doing so does nothing to blemish his reputation – and therefore his immortal soul.

We have no doubt, later, that when he expresses his horror at the killing of Duncan he is saying what he means and feels. Feelings have to be mastered before proper reasoned action is initiated:

> … when we have our naked frailties hid
> That suffer in exposure, let us meet
> And question this most bloody piece of work
> And know it further. Fears and scruples shake us.
> In the great hand of God I stand, and thence
> Against the undivulged pretence I fight
> Of treasonous malice.
>
> (Act II, scene 3, 123-29)

Reason and judgement are present in this speech, as are honour, uprightness, and integrity. We notice too yet another of those deferments of which the play is full – a past event felt in the present anticipating an event in the future. In the first scene of Act III, Banquo is given a soliloquy, which, on one hand, may be taken as an unguarded moment in which he is also seen to be tempted by the Weird Sisters' prophecies and, on the other, as an equivalent to Macbeth's earlier *che sarà sarà* posture – the one he adopted before he had to listen to Duncan's promotion of his son, Malcolm, as next in line to the throne. One thing is clear: he obviously harbours suspicions:

> Thou hast it now: King, Cawdor, Glamis, all
> As the weird women promised; and I fear
> Thou playest most foully for't. Yet it was said
> It should not stand in thy posterity
> But that myself should be the root and father
> Of many kings. If there come truth from them,
> As upon thee, Macbeth, their speeches shine,
> Why by the verities on thee made good
> May they not be my oracles as well
> And set me up in hope?
>
> (Act III, scene 1, 1-10)

This is Shakespeare strategically reminding the audience of the plot, so as to prepare it for the next major dramatic event: the assassination of Banquo. Once again, we are witnesses to a recapitulation of past events and a projection into the future with "if" and "may", "oracles" and "hope". The present is where past and future collide and, in the play, ultimately cancel themselves out. A Buddhist would tell us that we can never encounter the present moment unless we rid ourselves of attachment to the past through memory and to the future through desire.

Banquo is killed before there is any way we can know whether he – like Macbeth – intended – or might be pressured into so doing – to bring events about by direct intervention. However, the suspect word in his soliloquy is "shine" and there is also something suspicious in the way he shuts this speech down with "But hush! No more". Whether he is subject to temptation remains another of the play's ambiguities and may put a different light on the assertion that he, as an originator of the Stuart line, is whiter than white and some kind of martyr.

He and Macbeth start the play as almost equal partners in greatness; they are brothers-in-arms; they fight to the uttermost; they are highly praised and are promised (and given) rewards by the king they so strenuously serve; they share the experience of meeting the Weird Sisters; and they have heard what is individually promised each of them. In the course of things, however, they become opposites … as Macbeth and Duncan and Macbeth and Edward the Confessor are also opposites.

12

I Have Done The Deed

There is a tension between what happens in the imagination and what happens in reality. (It has often been pointed out that the disjunction between appearance and reality, made inherently dramatic by Shakespeare, is a central feature in all his plays). Macbeth's imagination is so potent, so wrought, that events become realer-than-real to him. The future floods in to the present. The visionary dagger is an obvious example of this. This tension causes time itself to collapse: the future (intention/desire backed by prediction – "I go and it is done") is experienced "in the instant"; the present is where action must occur but then, once done, the action/deed ("I have done the deed") enters the present as memory and makes the future forfeit, the present intolerable. The greatness of Lady Macbeth is that she can – at least in the beginning – shake her husband out of his mental/moral paralysis by making the future more seductive than "present imaginings". But not for long. Macbeth instantly and totally identifies himself with the murder ("To know myself, 'twere best not know my deed"). In the process he becomes "a man forbid".

It is also worth remarking that it is language itself that fuels Macbeth's mind and makes it feverish. In order to carry out the murder he has to tell it to shut up its chatter: "Words to the heat of deeds too cold breath gives". This is something felt also by Macduff when he and Macbeth finally confront each other at the end of the play:

> I have no words;
> My voice is in my sword, thou bloodier villain
> Than terms can give thee out.
>
> (Act V, scene 6, 45-7)

The "deed" is the most frightful of all crimes (Shakespeare's

50

audience would make no distinction between crime and sin): it is that of regicide. "Murder most foul, as in the best it is."

Macduff's reaction to the discovery of Duncan's murdered body is, for the time, the orthodox one:

> Confusion now hath made his masterpiece;
> Most sacrilegious murder hath broke ope
> The Lord's anointed temple and stole thence
> The life o'the building.

(Act II, scene 3, 63-6)

Leaving aside the question of whether this involves the Divine Right of Kings, what we have to register here is that Macduff's reaction is inevitably a religious one. Shakespeare has already much explored the business of regicide in his History Plays. In *Richard II* a king is described as being "God's deputy, anointed in his sight," In other words, kings were the highest in the hierarchical order of things; they were God's representatives on earth; and the killing of a legitimate king was an offence to God of the highest kind. Duncan's murder is "sacrilegious", his body is a "temple" (we may remember Macbeth's castle is ironically associated with the "temple-haunting martlet"), and, in the anointing ceremony, he has been legitimised by God and, as the "life o'the building", may be seen as being no less than his nation's soul. If, as we have suggested, the central exploration in the play is of the nature of a deed and its consequences (and therefore about conscience), then the deed at its epicentre is the worst imaginable. In John Wain's words:

> The crime of Macbeth is a shockingly multiple violation of
> *pietas*. Like Claudius, he commits murder, and the murder of
> a kinsman, in order to seize the throne. But his action throws
> an even darker shadow than Claudius'. As a host, he kills the
> guest who is depending on his protection. As a husband, he
> allows his wife to overrule him for an evil purpose. As a soldier
> enjoying the special gratitude of King and people for having
> saved them from a dangerous enemy, he tosses that gratitude
> aside by murdering the King and oppressing the people.

This is a useful summary but it misses out the fact that the crime is also the grossest of sins.

51

Act II, scene 1, ends with Macbeth's vision of the dagger. As if wielded by an invisible Bad Angel, it "marshall'st me the way that I was going". One cannot avoid the sexual implications in this speech in the allusion to "Tarquin's ravishing strides": the murder is being equated with rape.

The decisive sentence is "I go, and it is done". The word "done" here refers to an event that Macbeth has yet to do. The future has already mated with the past. Few other words in the play are used with so much resonance … including a sexual one.

13

Macbeth Shall Sleep No More

The murder of Duncan takes place in the middle of the night, almost certainly at the witching hour of midnight (the witches are referred to in Act IV, scene 1, as "secret, black, and midnight hags"). Macbeth vividly describes the hour:

> Nature seems dead, and wicked dreams abuse
> The curtained sleep. Witchcraft celebrates
> Pale Hecate's offerings; and withered Murder,
> Alarumed by his sentinel the wolf,
> Whose howl's his watch, thus with his stealthy pace,
> With Tarquin's ravishing strides, towards his design
> Moves like a ghost.
>
> (Act II, scene 1, 50-6)

This is not mere scene-painting, a wish to create poetic atmosphere, it is an expression of a widely-held belief – namely that night, blackness and evil were equated in the popular mind of the time. Remember too that the original audience had the strangeness of imagining these night scenes during afternoon performances at the open-air Globe.

What takes place, at the human (as distinct from the kingly) level, is the murder of a defenceless, weak, old man in his sleep. It is a cowardly act, ironically urged on by the accusation that not to perform it is cowardly. And the consequences are absolutely the reverse of what the Macbeths had hoped for: "I have done the deed" is a self-pronounced sentence, a sentence on himself. From now on Macbeth's total indentification with the deed locks him into an intolerable present in which all his senses are numbed. Lady Macbeth comes to inhabit the margins of his thoughts. Plotting Banquo's death, he tells his partner in greatness "Be innocent of the knowledge, dearest chuck, till thou applaud the deed" and from this moment on they are, in the words of Nicholas Brooke, "never intimate again; simultaneously their roles are reversed, and he now displays the determination on blood which was once hers alone, but which she can no longer sustain." (I am tempted to interpret the word "intimate" here as a Freudian slip: it would make sense to think of Macbeth as impotent or suddenly, traumatically losing his sexual drive).After doing the deed, Macbeth's self-image no longer needs her. The announcement of her death reveals to us a Macbeth whose feelings are totally atrophied. All he can manage is the pathetic (but poignant to the audience):

> She should have died hereafter.
> There would have been a time for such a word.
>
> (Act V, scene 5, 17-18)

This statement acts as introduction to the magnificently nihilistic poetry of what is the play's most famous speech, one in which what we have been saying about time and tenses reaches its climax:

> Tomorrow, and tomorrow, and tomorrow,
> Creeps in this petty pace from day to day
> To the last syllable of recorded time;
> And all our yesterdays have lighted fools
> The way to dusty death. Out, out, brief candle!
> Life's but a walking shadow, a poor player
> That struts and frets his hour upon the stage
> And then is heard no more. It is a tale
> Told by an idiot, full of sound and fury
> Signifying nothing.
>
> (Act V, scene 5, 19-28)

In Christian terms this is a full-blown expression of the sin of despair, the sin Donne feared in the last stanza of *A Hymne to God the Father*:

> I have a sinne of feare, that when I have spun
> My last thread, I shall perish on the shore.

It is also a terrifying expression of utter loneliness, of a man whose feelings become neutralised, a hero tangled in a net of his own making. As Kiernan Ryan puts it in his *Shakespeare*:

> The "imperfect speakers" of the heath can predict, but they cannot coerce. Within the historical bounds of his situation, as he is culturally constrained to perceive it, Macbeth's fate is the work of his own mortal hands.

An often-made contrast with Macbeth is Richard III. Both are villains but Richard is nearer to our conception of the pantomime villain who draws his audience into colluding in his mischief, whereas Macbeth is a compelling psychological portrait of a man tortured by conscience and seeking to numb its torment. Richard confides in us, makes us vicariously complicit; Macbeth suffers and we are helpless witnesses of his suffering. Both plays show us a rise and fall in fortunes, a contest between good and evil, the disruption of political order followed by the restoration of harmony and hope. We secretly admire, while publicly jeering, Richard's cheek; we enjoy his black humour and then righteously applaud his comeuppance. The focus in *Macbeth* is on what the two main characters are feeling and thinking and on the consequences of their actions and, in particular, on the self-destruction of the hero. To begin with Macbeth is caught up in something he doesn't fully understand. Richard III knows what he wants and gleefully plots it to attain his ends. There is nothing of the clown about Macbeth. He keeps dithering: he has a deep-seated moral sense that Richard lacks and he knows what the consequences of his actions are likely to be. But the temptation, especially heightened by his wife's sexual blackmailing, is too great for him. He has to fight against his gained successes in life and the social respect he has earned in the process. He is no pantomime villain but a mortal being with weaknesses, like the rest of us. In Roman Polanski's film of the play, the murder is shown to us and Polanski has Macbeth hesitating and Duncan waking: Macbeth has no alternative in the circumstances but to murder the King. It is a liberty taken by the director but one which makes an aspect of the play crystal clear. Macbeth is forced to propel what he has imagined into reality. As Ian Johnston says in his downloadable essay *An Introduction to Macbeth*:

Macbeth, in a sense, is tricked into murdering Duncan, but he tricks himself. That makes the launching of his evil career much more complex than a single powerful urge that produces a clear decision.

14

Murder Done On Banquo

The murder is an "allthing unbecoming". After the slaying of Duncan, Macbeth no longer needs to prove himself to his wife. He now assumes her role as organiser, is no longer the direct doer. In a sense, his will has been broken; his need for incentive is diminished. However, he seems to stoke himself up to murder Banquo and one wonders whether he is manufacturing self-justifications, proposing the event in the hope of stimulating his atrophied emotions or perhaps making a further gratuitous onslaught on fear itself:

> To be thus is nothing;
> But to be safely thus! – Our fears in Banquo
> Stick deep; and in his royalty of nature
> Reigns that which would be feared. 'Tis much he dares,
> And to that dauntless temper of his mind
> He hath a wisdom that doth guide his valour
> To act in safety. There is none but he
> Whose being I do fear.
>
> (Act III, scene 1, 47-54)

What reasons does he have for killing his friend? Does he realistically think he can thwart the witches' predictions when all the evidence so far has been that what they "promised" has come true? It is possible to claim he wants posterity (still expecting to father children) to belong to him and not to Banquo; that he knows Banquo suspects him of foul play; that he is conscious – as he himself admits – that what he has done has been done for nothing and that, instead of posterity, this nothing (i.e. inglorious oblivion) is his future. It is a word ("nothing") he will realise the truth of after hearing of the death of his wife. It is also, we may say in passing, a word used with enormous significance in *King Lear* (usually dated the same year of composition as *Macbeth*) where *all/some/nothing* are constantly being weighed in the balance. Whatever his motives, Macbeth is using Banquo as a focus for all his fears.

Now King, Macbeth orders a celebratory supper, which we are told will begin at 7pm. Banquo is publicly invited to be the chief guest. Ironically, his ghost fulfils this function for him. He and his son intend to go out riding and we are informed that this will involve their being out after dark – borrowers "of the night for a dark hour or twain". Once again, the motifs of night and horses are brought together. Macbeth interviews the murderers (note that this is for the *second* time) and tests their mettle by asking them where they think they fit in the hierarchical order of nature. As there are different degrees in the order of dogs, so there are in men:

> Now, if you have a station in the file,
> Not i'the worst rank of manhood, say't,
> And I will put that business in your bosoms,
> Whose execution takes your enemy off,
> Grapples you to the heart and love of us,
> Who wear our health but sickly in his life,
> Which in his death were perfect.
>
> (Act III, scene 1, 101-7)

He has become – doing the Devil's work for him – the tempter, the moral blackmailer: trying hard to suppress the feminine side of his nature, he has taken over his wife's role. She is now redundant.

He tells the murderers ("to your assistance making love") that it isn't politic for him to act on his own initiative. (I needn't point out the ironic resonances of the word "love".) And though he has stressed to them that it is Banquo who is their enemy, he insists on Fleance's death too. The Devil is a deceiver, an equivocator.

In the interim between this scene and the banquet, we overhear a short (two couplets) soliloquy of Lady Macbeth in which frustration is clearly evident:

> Nought's had, all's spent,
> Where our desire is got without content.
> 'Tis safer to be that which we destroy
> Than by destruction dwell in doubtful joy.
>
> (Act III, scene 2, 4-7)

58

In the conversation between her and Macbeth that follows she complains of neglect:

> How now, my lord? Why do you keep alone,
> Of sorriest fancies your companions making,
> Using those thoughts which should indeed have died
> With them they think on? Things without all remedy,
> Should be without regard; what's done, is done.
>
> (Act III, scene 2, 8-12)

and tries to cancel out the distance between them with her old, but now unavailing, argument that he should simply ignore what is troubling him. Her earlier words from Act II no longer have any persuasive power:

> The sleeping, and the dead
> Are but as pictures. 'Tis the eye of childhood
> That fears a painted devil.
>
> (Act II, scene 2, 53-5)

And her "what's done, is done" has quite a different meaning for him, one which she has no way of comprehending. It is this difference that inexorably represents the separation between them. Sleeplessness and the affliction of terrible dreams when asleep transform themselves into a death wish:

> Better be with the dead
> Whom we, to gain our peace, have sent to peace,
> Than on the torture of the mind to lie
> In restless ecstasy. Duncan is in his grave;
> After life's fitful fever he sleeps well;
> Treason has done his worst. Nor steel, nor poison,
> Malice domestic, foreign levy, nothing
> Can touch him further.
>
> (Act III, scene 2, 19-26)

Macbeth is envious of the sleep of the dead: better that than life's fitful fever and the evils attendant on it. His wife has no way of comprehending the depths of such despair. Her response:

> Come on,
> Gentle my lord, sleek o'er your rugged looks,
> Be bright and jovial among your guests tonight.
>
> (Act III, scene 2, 26-8)

albeit it elicits his "So shall I, love", evinces her impotence. Even when he comes out with "O, full of scorpions is my mind, dear wife!", she fails to understand the strength of his sufferings. And she is excluded from the plot to kill Banquo and Fleance. Again the indelible word "done" is used:

> Macbeth: ... there shall be done
>   A deed of dreadful note.
>
> Lady Macbeth: What's to be done?
>
> Macbeth: Be innocent of the knowledge, dearest chuck .
>
> (Act III, scene 2, 44-6)

and there is an obvious irony in the word "innocent". The gap between them is emphasized at the end of the scene when he says "Thou marvell'st at my words; but hold thee still." We may find ourselves asking: is he pathetically doing the deed to impress her? What, if anything, is implied in his invitation "So, prithee, go with me"?

15

But One Down

Nicholas Brooke's footnote in his introduction to *The Oxford Shakespeare* on the three murderers is sensible:

> Speculation about the identity of the Third Murderer (Macbeth himself, Destiny, etc.) is absurd: l. 2 fully explains his presence and is wholly in line with the dramatization of mistrust from 2.3 onwards.

In other words, whoever he is, he has been sent as spy to make sure (and this doesn't make his presence any less sinister) the other two do the business properly. Spying becomes part of Macbeth's rule, as he tells us later in Act III "There's not a one of them but in his house/ I keep a servant fee'd."

It is interesting to note the time of day. In his speech at the end of the previous scene, Macbeth had suggested the coming-on of night:

> Light thickens
> And the crow makes wing to the rooky wood;
> Good things of day begin to droop and drowse,
> Whiles night's black agents to their preys do rouse.
> (Act III, scene 2, 50-3)

The association with evil is conventional (one feels, throughout, the impact the play had on Blake). The second murderer informs us that "The west yet glimmers with some streaks of day"; we are also told that it is usual practice for people to dismount and walk the last mile to the castle.

In a confusion of light and dark (the stage direction states that the First Murder strikes out the light), the business is botched: "the son is fled" and "We have lost/ Best half of our affair". The word "lost" has obvious resonances and the scene ends with one more use of the fatal word "done":

> Well, let's away and say how much is done.
>
> (Act III, scene 3, 22)

16

Fail Not Our Feast

The Macbeth's banquet begins with "You know your own degrees, sit down". This is a clearly the expression of (a wished-for) order. The guests are to be seated according to their position in the hierarchical arrangement, a system that is not just social but cosmological. It is often said that order/disorder are central concerns in Shakepeare. Duncan's murder had been a breach in nature; the storm which automatically followed on from it is cataclysmic, a momentous breach in nature (apprehended as actual as well as poetic), in which strange inversions like Duncan's horses becoming cannibalistic, took place. Macbeth's banquet is designed by him in the hope his guests will see him as a restorer and sustainer of order. But the feast ends with Lady Macbeth's instructions to the guests to "Stand not upon the order of your going" and the accusation:

> You have displaced the mirth, broke the good meeting
> With most admired disorder.
>
> (Act III, scene 4, 108-9)

In other words, the hierarchical arrangement of the seated guests has been overturned. Hope of re-establishing order is deferred to the end of the play and is finally heard in Malcolm's line: "We will perform in measure, time, and place". Disruption of the natural order activates convulsions (storms, wars, mental turmoil) necessary to its re-establishment – socially, politically and cosmically.

The appearance of Banquo's ghost is an intensely theatrical event. In most productions a figure – which Macbeth and the audience see but his wife and guests do not – appears horrifyingly on stage. Some (for example Trevor Nunn's 1979 film) see the ghost as a self-projecting of Macbeth's guilty conscience, the audience sharing Lady

Macbeth's viewpoint when she insists "You look but on a stool". Whatever the interpretation, the original audience would have believed ghosts to be real and not imaginary. Represented on stage, shaking gory locks, or not, either way the effect is palpable. The past (a dead man) visits and is real in the present. It gives the lie to Lady Macbeth's perception of the sleeping and the dead as pictures and to Macbeth's wishful-thinking that, after life's fitful fever, the dead sleep well.

Ghosts to the original audiences were real enough but it was difficult for the audience (as it is for Hamlet) to fathom what guise they came in and what their purpose might be. They could be good spirits or evil or "perturbèd" spirits seeking revenge for some injustice done to them alive. As Hamlet declares on seeing the ghost of his father for the first time:

> Angels and ministers of grace defend us!
> Be thou a spirit of health or goblin damned,
> Bring thee airs from heaven or blasts from hell,
> Be thy intents wicked or charitable,
> Thou com'st in such questionable shape
> That I will speak with thee. I'll call thee Hamlet,
> King, father, royal Dane. O, answer me!
> Let me not burst in ignorance, but tell
> Why thy canonized bones, hearsèd in death,
> Have burst their cerements, why the sepulcher
> Wherein we saw thee quietly interred
> Hath oped his ponderous and marble jaws
> To cast thee up again. What may this mean
> That thou, dead corse, again in complete steel,
> Revisits thus the glimpses of the moon,
> Making night hideous, and we fools of nature
> So horridly to shake our disposition
> With thoughts beyond the reaches of our souls?
> Say, why is this? Wherefore? What should we do?
> (Act I, scene 4, 39-57)

Banquo's ghost manifests itself to Macbeth alone and makes sure that, by disrupting the feast, he continues to be isolated. And the ghost says nothing nor needs to – its appearance is accusation enough. Vengeance lies in other hands, those of Fleance, to whom his father addressed the dying words "Fly, good Fleance, fly, fly, fly! Thou mayst revenge", and Macduff. So the ghost, as well as being a walking accusation, is also prophetic: he is an aspect of that gathering energy that will bring about Macbeth's downfall.

Lady Macbeth's excuses for him are simply that: "The fit is momentary ... a thing of custom". They fail to save the situation. In a sense she has been displaced by the ghost: it is the ghost's unspoken accusations Macbeth attempts to counter in much the same mode as he had earlier responded to her:

> What man dare, I dare.
> Approach thou like the rugged Russian bear,
> The armed rhinoceros, or the Hyrcan tiger,
> Take any shape but that, and my firm nerves
> Shall never tremble. Or be alive again,
> And dare me to the desert with thy sword:
> If trembling I inhabit then, protest me
> The baby of a girl. Hence, horrible shadow!
> Unreal mockery, hence!
>
> (Act III, scene 4, 98-106)

We should be accustomed now to noticing the significant repetitions of words and the way they interweave themselves in the play's verbal texture. Here we have three "dare's" and a further reference to babies; Lady Macbeth, in this scene, has sought to explain her husband's shameful behaviour by pretending he has a medical condition (not the illness of ambition). His speech is again about manhood ("What man dare, I dare") and when the ghost finally makes his exit we hear Macbeth saying "Why, so; being gone,/ I am a man again" – words highly charged with irony for what we are looking at is an unmanned man, a shattered man. He now feels he has only one source of hope, of having any future. He will revisit the witches:

> I will tomorrow –
> And betimes I will – to the Weird Sisters.
> More shall they speak; for now I am bent to know
> By the worst means the worst. For mine own good
> All causes shall give way. I am in blood
> Stepped in so far, that, should I wade no more,
> Returning were as tedious as go o'er.

Strange things I have in head, that will to hand;
Which must be acted ere they may be scanned.

(Act III, scene 4, 131-9)

To his determination to harden himself:

>   My strange and self-abuse
> Is the initiate fear that wants hard use.
> We are yet but young in deed.

(Act III, scene 4, 141-3)

all his wife can say is you're not getting enough sleep.

17

Our Duties Did His Welcome Pay

This time Macbeth *visits* the witches, as opposed to being met by them, and does so as a man already stepped or steeped in blood. He is no longer the wide-eyed "innocent" of the first encounter. G.K. Hunter, in his Introduction to the New Penguin Shakespeare, makes the point that Macbeth:

> knows that his success is being bought by damnation, and he does not care. All he cares about is 'security' in what he does; in that case moral status becomes irrelevant; for then (III.4.20-22) he is:
>
> > perfect,
> > Whole as the marble, founded as the rock,
> > *As broad and general as the easing air* ...
> > (my emphasis)

But what is 'security'? Hecat reminds us (III.5.32-3) that:

> *you all know security*
> (my emphasis)
> Is mortals' chiefest enemy.

This is a useful reminder, for the word is one that has lost its relevant meaning. The *Oxford English Dictionary* tells us that it is '*archaic*: a culpable absence of anxiety'. The absence of anxiety was conceived to be culpable, because man may not be confident or 'secure' about the most important thing in life – his salvation. If he is 'secure', then it must be because the Devil has closed up his senses to the obvious and omnipresent dangers that everyone knew to lurk around the living – because he is in that state of sadness that theologians called 'despair'.

The scenes (Act III, scene 5 and Act IV, scene 1) have pre-echoes – most obviously in the earlier witches' appearance but also in the devil-portering scene. Macbeth's second encounter with the witches and Act II, scene 3, have the sound knocking (to admit sinners) in them, as well as a pageant of figures – albeit the porter's minatory procession is drawn from his cynical imagination, whereas things visible come out of the witches' cauldron. The porter gives us "a farmer, that hanged himself on the expectation of plenty", "an equivocator, that could swear in both the scales against either scale", "an English tailor ... for stealing out of a French hose", and he forebears to "let in some of all professions that go the primrose way to the everlasting bonfire". All of these mirror what goes on in the rest of the play. We have expectations of plenty indeed and a suicide; to repeat, the whole play is built around the notion of equivocation; the destination of sinners is advertised.

It is not of immediate interest here to detail the complications of the disputed authorship of these scenes. Brooke's Introduction to *The Oxford Shakespeare* provides a good enough account. The present purpose is to determine what is going on in the mind of Macbeth. But before we do this, there is a question we might pose – though we cannot expect an answer: is it Macbeth's decision (as he suggests to his wife) to consult the witches or has he been deluded into thinking it is? In other words, has he been summoned, drawn there by enchantments? Is he the victim of events already determined?

Act III, scene 5 opens with Hecat, whom H.J. Rose in *Gods and Heroes of the Greeks* describes as "a goddess originally Karian, of functions something like those of Artemis, with whom she is often confused; she later became the disreputable patroness of witches". According to Jenny March's *Dictionary of Classical Mythology* "she is often represented with three faces or three bodies".

Hecat berates the Three Sisters for playing fast and loose with the art of witchcraft so as to entrap someone of little significance:

> a wayward son,
> Spiteful and wrathful, who, as others do,
> Loves for his own ends, not for you.
>
> (Act III, scene 5, 11-13)

This is yet another of those scenes where a meeting takes place so as to determine a further one, where expectation displaces present reality:

> get you gone,
> And at the pit of Acheron
> Meet me i'the morning. Thither he
> Will come, to know his destiny.

(Act III, scene 5, 14-17)

Ironically, this projected next meeting is concerned with the future. One may imagine that morning in hell (Acheron is a river in hell) is black as night. There spirits are to be conjured:

> As by the strength of their illusion
> Shall draw him on to his confusion.

(Act III, scene 5, 28-9)

Is Macbeth at the mercy of fate? Or is he embracing it of his own volition?

Much of this is, to a modern audience, pantomimic, but can be, in the hands of an imaginative director (though few can resist making cuts of some kind), made to be terrifying and integral to the play, rather than something imported and foreign.

Before we meet the witches again there is a brief scene in which suspicions among the thanes are voiced, the first sentence of which tells us that there have already been previous conversations hinting at Macbeth's dodgy behaviour, and connection is made to probable future action in the mention of Macduff and Malcolm living among the English. Again the past is reported in the present in order to determine a future.

I am almost tempted to interpret Act IV, scene 1 as the equivalent of consulting a quack to supply Macbeth with an aphrodisiac. Perhaps it would be fairer to extend this more generally to stimulant, something to recharge his batteries. He is a walking dead man, looking for a resurgence of his manhood, a reconnecting with life; a man anxious to repossess a future. He is told in this scene to be "bloody, bold, and resolute." These are the very soldierly qualities we were asked to admire him for at the play's beginning and which he has subsequently perverted.

The witches' verse is appropriately banal and at the same time hypnotic, with its refrains, insistent rhymes, lists of gruesome bestial ingredients, the repetition of magic words like "thrice" and "double". They declare that they are to do a "deed without a name", which begs the question whether anything can exist without an identity. John Lucas has pointed out to me that Adam named the animals and therefore included them in God's kingdom; it was the nameless (bastards – see Edmund in *King Lear*) who stood outside grace and redemption. Their reply is a sinister one, one that resonates with all the permutations of the verb 'to do' that permeate the text. Brooke annotates the apparitions they conjure with: they "remain, as they undoubtedly should, cryptic, but it is true the sequence "armed head", "bloody babe", "crowned child holding a tree" (presumably of fertility) suggests a meaningful sequence through death to rebirth – from which Macbeth is excluded." This seems fair.

Macbeth is at the mercy of the witches and their grim provocations: in his submission to them he is unmanned to the extent that they require him to be quiet, telling him "Listen, but speak not", "Seek to know no more". And yet they seem to offer him what he was hoping for. The first set of apparitions, as Hecat had predicted, will cause him to "bear/ His hopes 'bove wisdom, grace, and fear." But the show of eight kings, though he does not fully know it, cancels out these hopes. No wonder, when they vanish, he demands:

> Where are they? Gone! Let this pernicious hour
> Stand aye accursed in the calendar.
>
> (Act IV, scene 1, 132-33)

18

Pernicious Hour

If one were to suggest a sub-title for our play, *Macbeth or the Tricks of Time* would not be too far off the mark – especially as we have been noticing how Time (in terms of tenses and the repetition of words like "hereafter", "tomorrow", "do", "done", "if", etc.) plays a major thematic role.

Shakespeare has already told us all the world's a stage where men and women play many parts. His theatre is, let's remember, called *The Globe* and he frequently enjoys making in-joke references to the theatre and its performing conditions – consistently so in *Hamlet* where, to give one example, he has Hamlet refer to the sky as "this brave o'erhanging firmament, fretted with golden fire" – an allusion to the ceiling above the apron stage painted with planets and stars. Players were called shadows: one of the most poignant puns in all Shakespeare's works is in Lear's referring to himself as "Lear's shadow". And Puck's epilogue to *A Midsummer Night's Dream*, begins with the words "If we shadows have offended".

In the wooden O of the Globe the audience is asked by the Prologue of *Henry V* to:

> … let us, ciphers to this great accompt,
> On your imaginary forces work.
> $\qquad$ (ll. 17-18)

and to think:

> … when we talk of horses, that you see them
> Printing their proud hooves i' th' receiving earth;
> For 'tis your thoughts that now must deck our kings,
> Carry them here and there, jumping o'er times,

Turning th' accomplishment of many years
Into an hourglass.

(ll. 26-31)

The word "ciphers" here, interestingly, signifies 'nothings'. Later
in this same play we are asked to "entertain conjecture of a time" –
in other words, we are to make what Coleridge famously called a
"willing suspension of disbelief". This means that chronological time
(Eliot's "the time of chronometers") is displaced by theatre-time
which allows for a certain ambivalence to operate.

We know we have come to witness a tragedy, expecting the acting-
out of the protagonist's downfall. Chaucer's *Monk's Tale* tells us:

Tragedie is to seyn a certeyn storie
As olde bokes make us memorie
Of him that stood in greet prosperitie
And is y-fallen out of heigh degree
Into miserie, and endeth wrecchedly.

Shakespeare's audience had similar expectations: to see a hero
driven to distraction and disaster. The 'lesson' enacted on stage was
often that tyrants never prosper.

But this expected outcome belongs to a conscious before and after,
to chronological time, whereas theatre-time allows, as we have
suggested, ambivalences. At the point of watching, things are more
complicated: our apprehension of many years is determined by the
turn of the hourglass; knowing what will happen, we have the
experience of wondering whether it will or not – or, more pertinently,
how it will. What I'm suggesting here is that perhaps we, too,
subconsciously entertain conjecture (at least half hope) that the
witches' predictions – that none of woman born can harm Macbeth
or that his downfall come about until Birnam Wood moves – may
still be a way out for him.

Ambivalence is at the heart of our experience of the play. If we
see the play as the personal tragedy of Macbeth, we cannot avoid
being moved by what Tillyard in *Shakespeare's History Plays* calls
"the discrepancy between his virtuous understanding and his corrupt
will". Nor can we fail to sympathise with Jan Kott's verdict that
Macbeth, after the appearance of Banquo's ghost, having "dreamed

of a final murder to end all murders, now 'knows: there is no such murder'". The "multiple murderer, steeped in blood, could not accept the world in which murder existed". Quoting an aphorism by S.J. Lec to the effect that "The sequence of time is an illusion ... We fear most the past that returns", he goes on to say:

> In this, perhaps, consists the gloomy greatness of this character, and the true tragedy of Macbeth's history. For a long time Macbeth did not want to accept the reality and irrevocability of nightmare, and could not reconcile himself to his part, as if it were somebody else's. Now he knows everything. He knows there is no escape from nightmare, which is the human fate and condition, or – in more modern language – the human situation.

Our sympathies are torn between how we feel witnessing the spectacle of an intensely suffering man, on whom time plays tricks, and the desire to underwrite the punishing of overweening ambition.

19

The Castle Of Macduff

With Act IV the play takes on a different rhythm. The three previous acts are characterised by compression and by a palpable darkness; now the play opens out on other perspectives, the landscape broadens, the air begins to sweeten a little. If the first three are more intimately domestic, the play now becomes more overtly political. The forces to oppose Macbeth begin to mass.

Central to these is Macduff, who, from Act IV on, is being groomed to become Scotland's saviour and the eventual executioner of Macbeth. Putting aside Shakespeare's source (Holinshed) for the moment, let's observe it is neither Fleance (because he is too young) nor the callow Malcolm who is designed to play the part of St. George to the Macbeth dragon.

Vengeance (Bacon's "wild justice") is part of Macduff's armoury. He is described by Ross as "noble, wise, and judicious" and as someone who "best knows/ The fits o' th' season". This is in answer to his wife's complaints that he has left her and his household unprotected. The slaughter of these is part of the preparation of the emergent hero. It provides necessary motivation but it also exposes another view of what it is to be manly. Lady Macduff's accusation "He loves us not,/ He wants the natural touch" seems to be spoken more out of vulnerability than conviction and in any case is later proved unjust. She is showing herself to be, in a conventional sense, womanly, in contrast to Lady Macbeth's unsexed womanliness. The assertion that her son "Fathered he is, yet fatherless" is something we can add to our list of seeming paradoxes that are part of the texture of the play. And we may note that the imagery of birds here (the "poor wren", the son as "poor bird") is set in contrast to the ominous black birds hovering over the action and is something echoed later in Macduff's "all my pretty chickens" hawked at and killed in one fell swoop by the hell-kite, Macbeth.

Lady Macduff is virtuous-minded:

> I have done no harm. But I remember now
> I am in this earthly world, where to do harm
> Is often laudable, to do good sometime
> Accounted dangerous folly. Why then, alas,
> Do I put up that womanly defence
> To say I have done no harm?
>
> (Act IV, scene 2, 74-9)

In her mouth "do" and "done" are restored to innocent use and the phrase "this earthly world" tells us that her thoughts have Eternity as their context. This is amplified by the reply she gives to the murderer who demands to know where her husband is:

> I hope in no place so unsanctified
> Where such as thou mayst find him.
>
> (Act IV, scene 2, 81-2)

(There is an anomaly here: Macbeth has been told by Lennox in the previous scene that "Macduff is fled to England" – why then does the murderer expect to find him at Fife – unless perhaps he thinks he may have returned?)

Macbeth's reasons for killing Macduff's family seem gratuitous but are in fact the outcome of the witches' telling him to beware the Thane of Fife and to be "bloody, bold, and resolute". His visit to them has renewed his energies:

> Time, thou anticipat'st my dread exploits.
> The flighty purpose never is o'ertook
> Unless the deed go with it. From this moment
> The very firstlings of my heart shall be
> The firstlings of my hand. And even now,
> To crown my thoughts with acts, be it thought and done:
> The castle of Macduff I will surprise,
> Seize upon Fife, give to the edge o' the sword
> His wife, his babes, and all unfortunate souls

That trace him in his line. No boasting, like a fool;
This deed I'll do before this purpose cool.

(Act IV, scene 1, 143-53)

This self-bolstering betrays a jealousy of Macduff – that he has a good wife and a family – while he himself has no son to assure him of genetic continuance, a connection into the future.

The following scene set in England represents Macduff's trial by ordeal – the feigned unworthiness of Malcolm and the news of the slaughter of his family and retainers. The first of these begins with an obvious irony:

> This tyrant, whose sole name blisters our tongues,
> Was once thought honest; you have loved him well;
> He hath not touched you yet.

(Act IV, scene 3, 12-14)

(We may wish to remember the word "touch" for its connection with the royal curative "touch" possessed by the English King: where this touch cures of the Evil, Macbeth's name alone is sufficient to blister the tongue).

Malcolm asks the question that so worried Lady Macduff:

> Why in that rawness left you wife and child,
> Those precious motives, those strong knots of love,
> Without leave-taking?

(Act IV, scene 3, 26-28)

His response suggests that Malcolm has hit a nerve: Macduff understands that there are higher loyalties to those of family. Loyalty to country comes first:

> Bleed, bleed, poor country!
> Great tyranny, lay thou thy basis sure,
> For goodness dare not check thee;

(Act IV, scene 3, 31-3)

The trial continues with Malcolm's pretence that he is a man too vicious to rule Scotland. His speeches deliver a parody of Macbeth's rule but in the process they delineate the "king-becoming graces" –

a list of qualities which we can use to measure the failings of all of Shakespeare's kings. Macduff passes the test: his purity of purpose is in no doubt; he can rightly stand as Scotland's champion. But a further test is in store.

Ross, at first unable to heave his heart into his mouth, finally informs Macduff of the murderous surprise of his castle. He is overwrought with grief and in response to Malcolm's urging that he "Dispute it like a man" says:

> I shall do so,
> But I must also feel it as a man.
>
> (Act IV, scene 3, 219-20)

This is a different kind of manliness from any we have so far met in the play, one that declares, however briefly, love and tenderness. I say however briefly because immediately we find him declaring:

> O, I could play the woman with mine eyes
> And braggart with my tongue! But, gentle heavens,
> Cut short all intermission. Front to front
> Bring thou this fiend of Scotland and myself
> Within my sword's length set him; if he scape,
> Heaven forgive him too.
>
> (Act IV, scene 3, 229-34)

Macduff's statement that Macbeth "has no children" not only means he has no pathway into futurity (as Macduff himself now no longer has – except, that is, through prowess, his fame as a warrior) but it also implies (despite the references to Heaven) that he has no children that can be part of a package of revenge ... or, perhaps, children that could take up the avenging of his death once Macduff has dealt it out.

Macduff has now emerged as the tried and tested saviour of Scotland, ready to put his voice into his sword.

20

Slumbery Agitation

"Glamis hath murdered sleep ... Macbeth shall sleep no more." It is obvious in any reading of the play that the motif of sleep runs importantly through it: the First Witch puts a charm on the "master o' the *Tiger*" which robs him of sleep; Banquo admits "A heavy summons lies like lead upon me,/ And yet I would not sleep"; Macbeth condemns himself to sleeplessness; Duncan is murdered in his sleep and is thought to "sleep well" after "life's fitful fever"; his guards are killed in "swinish sleep" ("There's one did laugh in his sleep,/ And one cried 'Murder'"); the porter declares sleep to be one of the things drink provokes; Lady Macbeth says of Duncan's murder "Had he not resembled my father as he slept, I'd done it"; she tells her husband that he lacks "the season of all natures, sleep"; Macduff calls sleep "death's counterfeit"; Lady Macbeth walks in her sleep.

Sleep is ambivalent: to the good and virtuous it is the season of all natures; it "knits up the ravelled sleeve of care": a favourite subject among Elizabethan sonneteers, Sidney's "Come, sleep, O sleep, the certain knot of peace", Daniel's "Care-charmer, Sleep, son of the sable Night" and, two hundred years later, Keats' "soft embalmer of the still midnight" that seals "the hushed Casket of my Soul". To the vicious it is a state of torment, a 'season' denied:

> Sleep shall neither night nor day
> Hang upon his penthouse lid.
> He shall live a man forbid.
>
> (Act I, scene 3, 19-21)

It is a territory vulnerable to invasion by evil spirits. The Doctor tells the Gentlewoman that "infected minds/ To their deaf pillows will discharge their secrets". "What dreams may come?" asks Hamlet.

Dreams, to Shakespeare's audience, came either from God or the Devil, in the form of curses being acted out or prophetic warnings. They were also nature's vengeance for the disruption brought about by evil. Macbeth knows that when nature "seems dead ... wicked dreams abuse/ The curtained sleep". Modern audiences, understandably, see the protagonists as revealing and being tortured by guilty consciences; they rarely perceive these things as operating in the context of Eternity.

"Macbeth shall sleep no more" – his is the torment of deprivation, the condition, as we have suggested earlier, of waking nightmare. Lady Macbeth's is a sleepwalking nightmare, which the Doctor describes, in Act V, scene 1, as a "great perturbation in nature, to receive at once the benefit of sleep and do the effects of watching" ("watching" meaning being awake). Macbeth's fate is to remain fully conscious; hers reveals that, for all her assumption of manly qualities, there is no defence against nature's retribution. According to Freud, she is "an example of a person who collapses on reaching success, after striving for it with single-minded energy ... a character which seemed forged from the toughest metal." He goes on to suggest:

> It would be a perfect example of poetic justice in the manner of talion if the childlessness of Macbeth and the barrenness of his Lady were the punishment for their crimes against the sanctity of generation – if Macbeth could not become a father because he had robbed children of their father and a father of his children, and if Lady Macbeth's illness, the transformation of her callousness into penitence, could be explained directly as a reaction to her childlessness, by which she is convinced of her impotence against the decrees of nature, and at the same time reminded that it is through her own fault if her crime has been robbed of the better part of its fruits.

(*The Shorter Oxford English Dictionary* gives *talion* as "the principle of exacting compensation, 'eye for eye, tooth for tooth'; also, the infliction of the same penalty on the accuser who failed to prove his case as would have fallen upon the accused if found guilty.")

It is certainly true that neither of them gains any satisfaction from becoming King and Queen. As early as Act III we hear her saying:

> Naught's had, all's spent,
> Where our desire is got without content.
> 'Tis safer to be that which we destroy
> Than by destruction dwell in doubtful joy.
>
> (Act III, scene 2, 4-7)

These lines may provide evidence for those who, like Kott, understand the sexual tensions that inform the play: words like "spent", "desire without content" suggest sexual disappointment as much as they do anything political. Let's remind ourselves of his words: "These two are sexually obsessed with each other, and yet have suffered a great erotic defeat". Freud is saying much the same thing – though he ignores the sexual blackmail that may be rooted in comparisons of performance (with a former husband by whom the historical Lady Macbeth had a child). The disappointment may simply be that Macbeth does not live up to her expectations in the bedroom. He certainly loses his drive – whether we put this down to simple ambition or not (what do you do next once you've climbed Everest?) – after he has murdered Duncan; and he certainly excludes her from things from then on.

Her sleepwalking dates from the time "his majesty went into the field" – the start for him of a progress back to the military arena whence he had come, covered with glory and blood, at the start of the play. Whatever it is that has separated them, separated and separate they are – pitifully isolated from each other and from the world. She was right: "Naught's had, all's spent".

With Duncan's blood on his hands, Macbeth had rhetorically asked himself:

> Will all great Neptune's ocean wash this blood
> Clean from my hand? No, this my hand will rather
> The multitudinous seas incarnadine,
> Making the green one red.
>
> (Act II, scene 2, 60-3)

at which point she comes back from having replaced the daggers – and therefore with proof of her complicity – with the words:

> My hands are of your colour; but I shame
> To wear a heart so white…

...
A little water clears us of this deed;

(Act II, scene 2, 68-70)

In the sleepwalking scene "It is an accustomed action with her, to seem thus washing her hands". This is Lady Macbeth's equivalent to the dagger scene, similarly stretching our imagination's sense of what is real. Is she possessed by evil spirits – invisible but real to the audience? The imagined blood she is attempting to scrub away (and which "all the perfumes of Arabia will not sweeten") is "damned" and associated with a vision of Hell as "murky". This religious context is strengthened by the Doctor's use of Lady Macbeth's earlier word "holily": "This disease is beyond my practice; yet I have known those that walked in their sleep, who have died holily in their beds" and his later verdict "More needs she the divine than the physician".

At the end of the scene Lady Macbeth brings to a climax all the previous uses of the word "done" with her statement "what's done, cannot be undone". And it is of no mean significance that her final words represent an invitation to her husband to come to bed ... to take "the primrose way to th' everlasting bonfire".

Her sleepwalking is both outside time and simultaneously within it; it is akin to the appearances of Banquo's ghost: she, like him, is an intrusion into the 'real' world of a different kind of reality, in a play, where 'reality' is like a set of Chinese boxes. Illusion and deception.

21

The English Power is Near

The pace quickens as the forces opposing Macbeth, led by Malcolm, Seyward and Macduff, begin to muster. "Revenges burn in them"; and we are told that their cause is "dear" – meaning both personal and honourable at the same time. There's an echo of Lady Macbeth's irremovable "damned spot" in Angus' mention of Macbeth's "secret murders sticking on his hands" and we learn that his men are disaffected: "Those he commands move only in command,/ Nothing in love".

When news of his wife's distraction reaches Macbeth, it comes as a total surprise, his senses are so numbed and his mind preoccupied with preparations for war. His fate (future) is advancing on him rapidly. As he admits in scene 5, just before hearing the news of her death:

> I have almost forgot the taste of fears.
> The time has been my senses would have cooled
> To hear a night-shriek, and my fell of hair
> Would at a dismal treatise rouse and stir
> As life were in't. I have supped full with horrors:
> Direness, familiar to my slaughterous thoughts,
> Cannot once start me.
>
> (Act V, scene 5, 9-15)

The only response to his wife's illness (of which he is clearly ignorant) he can give is to ask the Doctor:

> Canst thou not minister to a mind diseased,
> Pluck from the memory a rooted sorrow,
> Raze out the written troubles of the brain,

And with some sweet oblivious antidote
Cleanse the stuffed bosom of that perilous stuff
Which weighs upon the heart?

(Act V, scene 3, 40-5

It is a rhetorical question, proceeding from his state of spiritual numbness. He might just as well be referring to his own "illness". It is little wonder that the doctor's reply "Therein the patient/ Must minister to himself" is met with a mixture of impatience and impotence:

Throw physic to the dogs! I'll none of it –
Come, put mine armour on, give me my staff.

(Act V, scene 3, 46-7)

Panic is barely being kept at bay by the riddling prophecies of the witches. Dramatic irony is put to work when in the next scene the audience hears Malcolm's orders:

Let every soldier hew him down a bough
And bear't before him; thereby shall we shadow
The numbers of our host, and make discovery
Err in report of us.

(Act V, scene 4, 4-7)

The news of his wife's actual death finds Macbeth at his most despairing and nihilistic. Where is the "dearest partner of greatness" with whom he was once so eager to share things? He has not only forfeited the future but also the here-and-now. He is already a dead man.

The wood moves. In Wain's words, it "is a wonderful visual symbol of the great tide of Nature flowing over the scene of Macbeth's crime, bringing healing and renewal". Macbeth summons up his last energies:

I 'gin to be aweary of the sun,
And wish the estate o' the world were now undone –
Ring the alarum bell! Blow wind, come wrack,
At least we'll die with harness on our back.

(Act V, scene 5, 49-52)

The word "done" has turned into its impossible opposite. He imagines, as a backcloth to the coming events, wind and wrack – nature thrown into confusion. Shakespeare's age was haunted by visions of cosmic disorder. That of Richard Hooker in his *Laws of Ecclesiastical Polity I* published in 1594 is not untypical. He writes:

> Now if nature should intermit her course ... if those mother elements of the world ... should lose the qualities which they now have; if the frame of that heavenly arch erected over our heads should loosen and dissolve itself; if the moon should wander from her beaten way, the times and seasons of the year blend themselves by disordered and confused mixture, the winds breathe their last gasp, the clouds yield no rain, the earth be defeated of heavenly influence, the fruits of the earth pine away as children at the withered breasts of their mothers no longer able to yield them relief; what then would become of man himself?

Malcolm's army, in contrast to Macbeth's imaginings, is characterised by order:

> You, worthy uncle,
> Shall with my cousin, your right noble son,
> Lead our first battle. Worthy Macduff and we
> Shall take upon's what else remains to do,
> According to our order.
>
> (Act V, scene 6, 2-6)

The disruptions to the natural order wrought by the Macbeths, the storm consequent upon Duncan's death in which "the earth/ Was feverous and did shake", and the banquet in which an attempt to re-establish order fatally collapsed with Lady Macbeth's instruction to the guests that they "stand not upon the order of your going", now look to Malcolm and Macduff – with the help of the English – to be put right.

22

Affairs of Death

It is important not to forget the obvious: that this is a play about death and killing. It is steeped in blood. The verdict delivered by Malcolm on Macbeth at the end is that he is a butcher.

There are at least nine deaths – some reported, some acted on stage. Those we do not see are made vivid in highly concentrated language or are horrifyingly represented physically by the instruments responsible (bloody daggers, bloody hands).

In battle, killing – if God is on your side (or rather you are on the side of God) – is legitimate. The killer, who may have to sacrifice his own life in the process, is a righteous agent of God's justice. Macbeth's unseaming of Macdonald is deemed praiseworthy; and he goes on killing until, with the capture of the Thane of Cawdor, victory, against seeming odds, is achieved. Cawdor is summarily executed for treason. The interesting thing in the report Malcolm gives of Cawdor's death is that he dies virtuously. This has to be seen as a compliment to Duncan (that "he confessed his treasons,/ Implored your highness' pardon") as well as a confirmation of the rightness of Duncan's cause. But more than that: it is important for us to understand that the state of the soul at the point of death determines its destination. Macbeth acknowledges this before he makes his way to Duncan's chamber:

> I go, and it is done; the bell invites me.
> Hear it not, Duncan, for it is a knell
> That summons thee to heaven, or to hell.
>
> (Act II, scene 1, 62-4)

Similarly, after briefing the murderers, he states:

It is concluded! Banquo, thy soul's flight,
If it find Heaven, must find it out tonight.

(Act III, scene 1, 140-1)

These are not rhetorical flourishes; to the Shakespeare's audience they are facts. (It is worth noting the expressions "I go and it is done" and "It is concluded" and their ironic connection back to "If it were done when 'tis done" – beneath the primary meaning of "done" and "concluded" there is the paradoxical sense of a future event brought into the present with a past tense).

Banquo dies on stage – albeit in darkness ("Who did strike out the light?") – in a torrent of stabbings ("twenty trenchèd gashes on his head") but continues to exist as a ghost. Macbeth – for whom killing on the battlefield is part of the job-description and not therefore a matter of conscience – is forced to admit:

The times has been
That, when the brains were out, the man would die,
And there an end. But now they rise again
With twenty mortal murders on their crowns,
And push us from our stools.

(Act III, scene 4, 77-81)

The slaughter of the virtuous Lady Macduff, her children and servants is, in the words of the messenger who comes to warn her of disaster, "fell cruelty" (Shakespeare's audience might well have linked in their minds with Herod and the slaughter of the Innocents). There is no other way of seeing it than as a heinous and, to some degree, gratuitous event. A gruesome parallel may be perhaps found in the ingredients that go into the cauldron, most of them pieces of animals killed for malicious purpose.

The death of the wicked Lady Macbeth comes as a shock, (more of a shock to us than to Macbeth), bleakly reported in the statement "The Queen, my lord, is dead". Later, it is suggested that she "by self and violent hands/ Took off her life". The unlawful death of anyone – be it murder or suicide – is a hubristic act. It is for God to decide when a person's death is to occur. To override Providence is to commit the sin of presumption. Suicides went to hell. That said, we only have Malcolm's supposition, with its rider "as 'tis thought" that Lady Macbeth killed herself. The verdict must remain an open one: she may well have, in her sleepwalking, tripped and tumbled down the stairs! It is worth noting that her husband first thinks of, then rejects, suicide as a way out – he has in mind the soldier's honourable exit by falling on his sword (as Brutus and Antony bunglingly do) i.e. performing execution upon themselves:

> Why should I play the Roman fool and die
> On mine own sword? Whiles I see lives, the gashes
> Do better upon them.
>
> (Act V, scene 6, 40-2)

Macbeth, like a great bull, is brought into the arena for his moment of truth.

The first to confront him is young Seyward. The bull gores him fatally. But it is through Seyward that honour can be foregrounded once again and a further gloss given to the idea of manliness. Though young, Seyward's son pays "a soldier's debt" and:

> … only lived but till he was a man;
> The which no sooner had his prowess confirmed
> In the unshrinking station where he fought
> But, like a man, he died.
>
> (Act V, scene 6, 79-82)

Again the theme of fathers and sons is pointed up. Seyward's father asks "Had he his hurts before?" and is told "Ay, on the front", to which he replies:

> Why then, God's soldier be he.
> Had I as many sons as I have hairs
> I would not wish them a fairer death.
>
> (Act V, scene 6, 86-8)

I am tempted to say that with his "Had I … I would not …" construction Old Seyward restores a proper dignity to the conditional tense.

There is no doubt in Macduff's mind as to what Macbeth's deserved destination is to be when finally granted the wish made at the end of Act IV:

Front to front
Bring thou this fiend of Scotland and myself.
Within my sword's length set him.

                              (Act IV, scene 3, 231-33)

"Turn hell-hound, turn!" he shouts. The sight of Macduff cows Macbeth's "better part of man" and at first he refuses to fight him. There is no boast but rather regret in the words:

Of all men else I have avoided thee.
But get thee back; my soul is too much charged
With blood of thine already.

                              (Act V, scene 6, 43-5)

Then, like the great bull in the bull-ring, Macbeth is brought to his knees and all that is now needed is his execution, the matador's sword, the moment of truth. But before doing so, Macduff cuts through Macbeth's final, tenuous hold on hope:

Despair thy charm,
And let the angel whom thou still has served
Tell thee Macduff was from his mother's womb
Untimely ripped.

                              (Act V, scene 6, 52-5)

Macbeth has relied on prophecies that turn out to be sick jokes, the cruellest of quibbles – in a word, equivocations. The invisible witches hovering over the scene are cackling inaudibly.

He summons up all the animal energy left to him for one final fling:

Yet I will try the last. Before my body
I throw my warlike shield. Lay on, Macduff;
And damned be him that first cries, 'Hold, enough!'

                              (Act V, scene 6, 71-3)

Already at the beginning of this scene he had described himself in terms of a baited animal:

They have tied me to the stake, I cannot fly,
But bear-like I must fight the course.

$$\text{(Act V, scene 6, 11-12)}$$

When he is dispatched and his head brought in (we remember the fate of Macdonald, whose head Macbeth fixed on the battlements) we know that he has at least died with harness on his back and can say that in doing so he had regained something of his warrior status. Whatever else we may think, we can recover the word "brave" for him.

23

The Time Is Free

Malcolm sums up the prosecution's case in the line "this dead butcher and his fiend-like queen", consigning both of them to history in the promise of a new order and virtuous governance:

> by the grace of Grace
> We will perform in measure, time, and place.
> So thanks to all at once, and to each one,
> Whom we invite to see us crowned at Scone.
>
> (Act V, scene 6, 111-14)

The double use of the word "grace" re-affirms the continuation of God's benediction, already granted in the alliance with the English and their pious king.

The restoration of order in Shakespeare's tragedies is always done snappily (think of the businesslike conclusions to plays like *Hamlet*, *Othello*). Those left behind to pick up the pieces are often pallid figures compared to the ones on which we have been focusing our attentions. Modern productions tend not to like closure and find some way of suggesting that the looked-forward-to future is an illusion. For example Malcolm and Macduff exchange looks that imply distrust – or Donalbain (Shakespeare has forgotten him) is re-introduced and similar fearful looks pass between him and his brother.

We are not, if we are honest, altogether concerned with these people: we are still thinking about Macbeth. The audience is a jury about to retire. They know that, even with all the murders sticking on his hands, there are still yes-buts and if-onlys hanging in the air. If we leave the theatre thinking good riddance to bad rubbish then we have, to use the words of T.S. Eliot, had the experience but missed the meaning. What we should be carrying away are ambivalent thoughts and feelings, uppermost among which must inevitably be an enormous sense of the loss of a great potential:

> Had I but died an hour before this chance
> I had lived a blessèd time; for from this instant
> There's nothing serious in mortality.
> All is but toys, renown and grace is dead,
> The wine of life is drawn, and the mere lees
> Is left this vault to brag of.
>
> (Act II, scene 3, 88-93)

Albeit this is Macbeth publicly averting attention from himself when Duncan's murder is discovered, it is a statement of central importance to the play. The construction is again conditional ("Had I ...") All the way through, he has been an *if*-man, a man with scruples (which his wife interpreted as dithering) and he has had to learn, to use words of Eliot's again, that:

> If all time is eternally present
> All time is unredeemable.

Time for him is consciousness shaped by conscience – the eternal presence of guilt creates a living hell which he has had to inhabit from the moment of his encounter with the witches. Does his death release him from time-as-consciousness or is this prolonged beyond the grave? We have seen ghosts and know that the play cannot work without an awareness of the context of Eternity; and we know that events in this life are not the "be-all and the end-all – here". In a sense Macbeth shows us what it is to be morally alive and what happens when human beings (think of Faustus who explores the tension between human aspiration and human limitation) dare.

There is no questioning his guilt. But is Macbeth redeemable in a higher court? Can God forgive even him?

He is a man who, like Othello, "being wrought" was "perplexed in the extreme". The witches opened up the pathway to temptation: he immediately finds himself torn between ambition and his moral sense; his formidable wife sexually blackmails him. One could argue that he is tricked into damnation or at least pressured into it against his better nature. All along he is tortured by the notion of wrong-doing. What the audience has been witnessing is a man pitiably suffering. It would be a callous or vicious member of the audience who did not feel 'there but for the grace of God go I'. In the process, Macbeth is stripped of everything, becomes a "walking shadow", or, in Lear's words, a "bare forked animal" with only physical energy left.

But he goes down fighting and isn't there part of us that admires this? Is he a good man gone wrong? Is this the reason we feel the loss of a great potential? At the conclusion of tragic works we cannot escape the feeling that something 'big' has gone out of life and that, in terms of potentiality, the world is an emptier and duller place. As the Chorus to Anouilh's *Antigone* puts it:

> In a tragedy, nothing is in doubt and everyone's destiny is known. That makes for tranquillity. There is a sort of fellow-feeling among characters in tragedy: he who kills is as innocent as he who gets killed: it's all a matter of what part you're playing. Tragedy is restful; and the reason is that hope, that foul, deceitful thing, has no part in it. There isn't any hope. You're trapped. The whole sky has fallen on you, and all you can do about it is shout. Don't mistake me: I said "shout": I did not say groan, whimper, complain. That, you cannot do. But you can shout out loud; you can get all those things said you'd never thought you'd be able to say – or never knew you had it in you to say. And you don't say these things because it will do any good to say them: you know better than that. You say them for their own sake; you say them because you learn a lot from them.

> In melodrama, you argue and struggle in the hope of escape. That is vulgar; it's practical. But in tragedy, where there is no temptation to try to escape, the argument is gratuitous: it's kingly.

The fact is Macbeth explores his potential for evil rather than for good.

Can we extend extenuations to the fiend-like queen? To do so we would need to identify her as victim. We have suggested that, for all her determined masculinity, she has a clearly repressed feminine nature which betrays itself in the observation "Had he not resembled my father as he slept" and in busying herself with the 'easier' role of organiser. The question 'Is she all talk?' was posed. Does the fact that she cracks first (was her fainting in Act II, scene 3 a put-on affair or already an indication of instability?) confirm this view? Should we use the insights of modern psychology to help us interpret her character in terms of repression and guilt or take the view that her sleepwalking is God's punishment, her suicide (if that's what it is) sending her pell-mell to hell? Is she 'just as human' as her partner or more irredeemably culpable than he? Freud found himself at a loss:

> And now we ask ourselves what it is that broke this character which seemed forged from the toughest metal? Is it only disillusionment – the different aspect shown by the accomplished – and are we to infer that even in Lady Macbeth an originally gentle and womanly nature had been worked up to a concentration and high tension which could not endure for long, or ought we to seek for signs of a deeper motivation which will make this collapse more humanly intelligible to us?

> It seems to me impossible to come to any decision.

But he goes on to offer an interesting view stimulated by his reading of a study of Shakespeare by Ludwig Jekels, who believed "that Shakespeare often splits a character into two personages", neither of which, taken separately, is "completely understandable and do not become so until they are brought once more into a unity". Applying this idea to the Macbeths, Freud suggests that:

> … the germs of fear which break out in Macbeth on the night of the murder do not develop further in *him* but in *her*. It is he who has the hallucination of the dagger before the crime; but it is she who afterwards falls ill of a mental disorder. It is he who after the murder hears the cry in the house: "Sleep no more! Macbeth does murder sleep … "; but we never hear that *he* slept no more, while the Queen, as we see, rises from her bed and, talking in her sleep, betrays her guilt. It is he who stands helpless with bloody hands, lamenting that "all great Neptune's ocean" will not wash them clean, while she comforts him:: "A little water clears us of this deed"; but later it is she who washes her hands for a quarter of an hour and cannot get rid of the bloodstains: "All the perfumes of Arabia will not

sweeten this little hand." Thus what he feared in his pangs of conscience is fulfilled in her; she becomes all remorse and he all defiance. Together they exhaust the possibilities of reaction to the crime, like two disunited parts of a single physical individuality, and it may be that they are both copied from the same prototype.

Then again there is the view that, in Johnston's words, her "lack of will to confront fully the consequences of her and Macbeth's actions makes her story one without the tragic significance of her husband's".

In a play so rich in ambiguities and ambivalence the field of interpretation is wide open. G.B. Harrison (quoted in the Macmillan Casebook) thinks the play "extravagantly over-praised", the "weakest of the great tragedies"; John Masefield calls it the "most glorious of Shakespeare's works". No single interpretation is ever 'right'; by the same token we are not to suppose that some of them cannot be wrong. To quote John Wain again:

> In studying a writer as many-sided as Shakespeare, a critic must take an account of *everything*.

This is, as the miles of shelves of Shakespearean criticism aptly show, an impossible task. More to the point is the need to keep renewing our acquaintance with Shakespeare and his plays and to do so in the spirit of Sir Simon Rattle as he expressed it in an interview with the BBC *Music Magazine* (April 2003). Asked why he had recorded a new cycle of the Beethoven symphonies when so many were already available, his answer was "We go on hurling ourselves at Beethoven and Shakespeare – we are destined to fail, but we're determined to make the best possible failure".

Bibliography

Jean Anouilh, *Antigone* (Methuen Modern Plays, 1960)

Jonathan Bate, *The Genius of Shakespeare* (Picador, 1997)

Harold Bloom, *Shakespeare: the Invention of the Human* (Fourth Estate, 1999)

A.C. Bradley, *Shakespearean Tragedy* (Macmillan, 1904)

Marchette Chute, *Shakespeare of London* (Four Square, 1962)

Samuel Taylor Coleridge, *Shakespearean Criticism* (2 vols.) edited by T.M. Raysor (Dent, 1960)

W. Croft Dickinson, *Scotland from Earliest Times to 1603*, third edition, revised and edited by A.A.M. Duncan (OUP, 1977)

W.C. Croft Dickinson, Gordon Donaldson, Isabel A. Milne, *A Source Book of Scottish History* (2 vols.) (Nelson, 1952)

John Donne, *The Complete English Poems* edited by C.A. Patrides (Dent, 1985)

Terry Eagleton, *William Shakespeare* (OUP, 1987)

T.S. Eliot, *Collected Poems and Plays* (Faber, 1969)

Antonia Fraser, *Mary Queen of Scots* (Weidenfeld & Nicholson, 1969)

Sigmund Freud, 'Some Character Types Met with in Psycho-analytical Work' in *Shakespeare's Macbeth* (Macmillan Casebook Series) edited by John Wain (1968)

George Herbert, *The Complete English Poems* edited by C.A. Patrides (Dent, 1974)

Anthony Holden, *William Shakespeare: His Life and His Work* (Abacus, 1999)

R.W. Holder (ed.) *The Faber Dictionary of Euphemisms* (Faber, 1989)

Ian Johnston, *An Introduction to Macbeth* English 366: Studies in Shakespeare (www.mala.bc.ca/~johnstoi/eng366/lectures/macbeth.htm)

L.C. Knights, *How Many Children Had Lady Macbeth?* (Folcroft Library Editions, 1933)

Some Shakespearean Themes and an Approach to Hamlet
(Peregrine, 1966)

Jan Kott, *Shakespeare Our Contemporary* (Methuen, 1964)

Jenny March, *Dictionary of Classical Mythology* (Cassell, 1998)

Sir Ian McKellen interviewed in *The Times* 17th February 2003

Thomas Norton and Thomas Sackville, *Gorboduc* in *Five Elizabethan Tragedies* (OUP, 1950)

Robert Nye, *The Late Mr Shakespeare* (Alison & Busby, 1997)

Roger Penrose, *The Emperor's New Mind – concerning computers, Minds and the Laws of Physics* (OUP, 1989)

Sir Simon Rattle interviewed in *BBC Music Magazine* April 2003

H.J. Rose *Gods and Heroes of the Greeks* (New English Library, 1974)

A.L. Rowse *Shakespeare the Elizabethan* (Weidenfeld & Nicholson 1977)

Kiernan Ryan, *Shakespeare* (Palgrave, 2001)

Caroline Spurgeon, *Shakespeare's Imagery & What It Tells Us* (CUP, 1935)

Alan Stewart, *The Cradle King* (Chatto & Windus, 2003)

E.M.W. Tillyard, *The Elizabethan World Picture* (Chatto & Windus, 1943)

Shakespeare's History Plays (Peregrine, 1962)

G.M. Trevelyan, *English Social History* (Pelican, 1967)

John Wain *The Living World of Shakespeare* (Pelican, 1966)

Shakespeare Macbeth (Macmillan Casebook Series, 1968)

Alexander Walker, *The Life of Vivien Leigh* (Grove Press, 1987)

Ann Williams, Alfred P. Smyth, D.P. Kirby, *A Biographical Dictionary of Dark Age Britain England, Scotland, Wales c. 500 to c.1050* (Seaby, 1991)

Hilary Lloyd Yewlett, *Macbeth and its Celtic Origins* (www.jmucci.com/ER/articles/yewlett.htm)

Editions used:

The *New Penguin Shakespeare* edited by G.K. Hunter and the introduction to *The Oxford Shakespeare* by Nicholas Brooke.

GREENWICH EXCHANGE BOOKS

Greenwich Exchange Student Guides are critical studies of major or contemporary serious writers in English and selected European languages. The series is for the student, the teacher and 'common readers' and is an ideal resource for libraries. The *Times Educational Supplement* praised these books, saying, "The style of these guides has a pressure of meaning behind it. Students should learn from that ... If art is about selection, perception and taste, then this is it."

(ISBN prefix 1-871551- applies)
The series includes:
W.H. Auden by Stephen Wade (36-6)
Honoré de Balzac by Wendy Mercer (48-X)
William Blake by Peter Davies (27-7)
The Brontës by Peter Davies (24-2)
Robert Browning by John Lucas (59-5)
Samuel Taylor Coleridge by Andrew Keanie (64-1)
Joseph Conrad by Martin Seymour-Smith (18-8)
William Cowper by Michael Thorn (25-0)
Charles Dickens by Robert Giddings (26-9)
John Donne by Sean Haldane (23-4)
Ford Madox Ford by Anthony Fowles (63-3)
Thomas Hardy by Sean Haldane (35-1)
Seamus Heaney by Warren Hope (37-4)
Philip Larkin by Warren Hope (35-8)
Laughter in the Dark – The Plays of Joe Orton by Arthur Burke (56-0)
Philip Roth by Paul McDonald (72-2)
Shakespeare's Non-Dramatic Poetry by Martin Seymour-Smith (22-6)
Shakespeare's Othello by Matt Simpson (71-4)
Shakespeare's Sonnets by Martin Seymour-Smith (38-2)
Tobias Smollett by Robert Giddings (21-8)
Alfred, Lord Tennyson by Michael Thorn (20-X)
William Wordsworth by Andrew Keanie (57-9)

cont'd...

98

Liar! Liar!: Jack Kerouac – Novelist
R.J. Ellis
The fullest study of Jack Kerouac's fiction to date. It is the first book to devote an individual chapter to every one of his novels. *On the Road, Visions of Cody* and *The Subterraneans* are reread in-depth, in a new and exciting way. *Visions of Gerard* and *Doctor Sax* are also strikingly reinterpreted, as are other daringly innovative writings, like 'The Railroad Earth' and his "try at a spontaneous *Finnegan's Wake*" – *Old Angel Midnight*. Neglected writings, such as *Tristessa* and *Big Sur*, are also analysed, alongside better-known novels such as *Dharma Bums* and *Desolation Angels*.
R.J. Ellis is Senior Lecturer in English at Nottingham Trent University.
1999 • 295 pages • ISBN 1-871551-53-6

BIOGRAPHY

The Good That We Do
John Lucas
John Lucas' book blends fiction, biography and social history in order to tell the story of his grandfather, Horace Kelly. Headteacher of a succession of elementary schools in impoverished areas of London, 'Hod' Kelly was also a keen cricketer, a devotee of the music hall, and included among his friends the great Trade Union leader, Ernest Bevin. In telling the story of his life, Lucas has provided a fascinating range of insights into the lives of ordinary Londoners from the First World War until the outbreak of the Second World War. Threaded throughout is an account of such people's hunger for education, and of the different ways government, church and educational officialdom ministered to that hunger. *The Good That We Do* is both a study of one man and of a period when England changed, drastically and forever.
John Lucas is Professor of English at Nottingham Trent University and is a poet and critic.
2001 • 214 pages • ISBN 1-871551-54-4

In Pursuit of Lewis Carroll
Raphael Shaberman
Sherlock Holmes and the author uncover new evidence in their investigations into the mysterious life and writing of Lewis Carroll. They examine published works by Carroll that have been overlooked by previous commentators. A newly discovered poem, almost certainly by Carroll, is published here.

Amongst many aspects of Carroll's highly complex personality, this book explores his relationship with his parents, numerous child friends, and the formidable Mrs Liddell, mother of the immortal Alice. Raphael Shaberman was a founder member of the Lewis Carroll Society and a teacher of autistic children.

1994 • 118 pages • illustrated • ISBN 1-871551-13-7

Musical Offering
Yolanthe Leigh

In a series of vivid sketches, anecdotes and reflections, Yolanthe Leigh tells the story of her growing up in the Poland of the 30s and the Second World War. These are poignant episodes of a child's first encounters with both the enchantments and the cruelties of the world; and from a later time, stark memories of the brutality of the Nazi invasion, and the hardships of student life in Warsaw under the Occupation. But most of all this is a record of inward development; passages of remarkable intensity and simplicity describe the girl's response to religion, to music, and to her discovery of philosophy.

Yolanthe Leigh was formerly a Lecturer in Philosophy at Reading University.

2000 • 57 pages • ISBN: 1-871551-46-3

Norman Cameron
Warren Hope

Norman Cameron's poetry was admired by W.H. Auden, celebrated by Dylan Thomas and valued by Robert Graves. He was described by Martin Seymour-Smith as, "one of ... the most rewarding and pure poets of his generation ..." and is at last given a full length biography. This eminently sociable man, who had periods of darkness and despair, wrote little poetry by comparison with others of his time, but always of a consistently high quality – imaginative and profound.

2000 • 221 pages • illustrated • ISBN 1-871551-05-6

POETRY

Adam's Thoughts in Winter
Warren Hope

Warren Hope's poems have appeared from time to time in a number of literary periodicals, pamphlets and anthologies on both sides of the Atlantic. They appeal to lovers of poetry everywhere. His poems are brief, clear, frequently lyrical, characterised by wit, but often distinguished by tenderness.

The poems gathered in this first book-length collection counter the brutalising ethos of contemporary life, speaking of and for the virtues of modesty, honesty and gentleness in an individual, memorable way.
2000 • 47 pages • ISBN 1-871551-40-4

Baudelaire: Les Fleurs du Mal
Translated by F.W. Leakey
Selected poems from *Les Fleurs du Mal* are translated with parallel French texts and are designed to be read with pleasure by readers who have no French as well as those who are practised in the French language.
F.W. Leakey was Professor of French in the University of London. As a scholar, critic and teacher he specialised in the work of Baudelaire for 50 years and published a number of books on the poet.
2001 • 153 pages • ISBN 1-871551-10-2

Lines from the Stone Age
Sean Haldane
Reviewing Sean Haldane's 1992 volume *Desire in Belfast*, Robert Nye wrote in *The Times* that "Haldane can be sure of his place among the English poets." This place is not yet a conspicuous one, mainly because his early volumes appeared in Canada and because he has earned his living by other means than literature. Despite this, his poems have always had their circle of readers. The 60 previously unpublished poems of *Lines from the Stone Age* – "lines of longing, terror, pride, lust and pain" – may widen this circle.
2000 • 53 pages • ISBN 1-871551-39-0

Wilderness
Martin Seymour-Smith
This is Martin Seymour-Smith's first publication of his poetry for more than twenty years. This collection of 36 poems is a fearless account of an inner life of love, frustration, guilt, laughter and the celebration of others. He is best known to the general public as the author of the controversial and bestselling *Hardy* (1994).
1994 • 52 pages • ISBN 1-871551-08-0